American Policing in 2022

Essays on the Future of a Profession

Edited by Debra R. Cohen McCullough
and Deborah L. Spence

COMMUNITY ORIENTED POLICING SERVICES
U.S. DEPARTMENT OF JUSTICE

"...service to the community is at the heart of everything every police officer should do, both now and in the future."

September 2012

★ ★ ★

Introduction

by Debra R. Cohen McCullough
and Deborah L. Spence

During a presentation to the American Society of Criminology in 2011, Jim Bueermann displayed a PowerPoint slide with this prediction: by 2022, every police department will have a resident criminologist. This got chuckles in the room, but later that week, as the two of us talked about Bueermann's prediction over lunch, we found we were intrigued by the idea of what predictions for policing other people might make for the next 10 or 20 years.

Initially, we thought we might use this idea of predicting the future to run a series of interviews for the *Community Policing Dispatch*, the e-newsletter for the Office of Community Oriented Policing Services (COPS Office). But the more we discussed it with co-workers, we realized the idea had the potential to be more powerful as a single, print collection than as a web-based series spanning a number of months. As a result, the idea for this book—that law enforcement leaders across the country could share their perspectives on what policing might/could/should look like 10 years from now—was born.

Who should we invite to join us in this project? This was the hardest part of the whole enterprise. For every one name we could think of, there were no doubt 10 we didn't know about. As excited as we were to embark on this project, we knew it would be a challenge to solicit essays from busy people with busy schedules with no monetary reimbursement and not even the promise of being published. Our current director, Bernard Melekian, was an obvious choice.

This book is the collected wisdom of 27 artists.

*   *   *

So too was Bueermann, considering that without his PowerPoint slide we would not have been inspired to create this at all. From there we talked to colleagues, read articles, paid attention to speakers we heard at meetings and conferences, and considered the types and sizes of agencies and organizations we felt needed to be represented, thus building a list of people we thought might work.

But would those we invited find the project as interesting as we did and want to participate? Luckily for us, they did. We have contributions from chiefs and former chiefs, as well as captains, lieutenants, a sergeant, an officer, and even a few who have made careers out of helping the police do their jobs better. They represent big cities, small towns, and tribal and state agencies. Some are already nationally known, others now will be, and all were gracious in giving their time and ideas to this project.

We gave the contributors little instruction on what to write. We simply asked them to share their view on the future of policing, presenting this as a chance for them to articulate their vision and, we hope, help shape the thinking of law enforcement professionals and policymakers alike. We then sat back and nervously waited for the essays to arrive. Unavoidably influenced from our years managing programs designed to propel policing into the 21st century, we predicted that essays on technology would dominate the submissions, followed quickly by talks of streamlining finances and keeping up with local economies. And we worried that the collection might trend toward everything we *wouldn't* be able to do in the future.

After the first few submissions, we realized our contributors were going to exceed our expectations. Important questions were being asked and answered about the core mission of police work, the ideal characteristics of leaders, the role of the community, the impact of the economy, and the measures of success. Ultimately, we selected a collection of honest, inspiring, and, in fact, quite personal essays on how the policing field can build on what we know now to create a better future.

We also worried about what we'd do if two people contributed the same idea. That didn't happen. While themes emerged among the essays, they were not repetitive. True, policing leaders appear to love quoting the father of modern policing, Sir Robert Peel, with seven essays referring to one or more of his nine principles. Similarly, James Q. Wilson and George Kelling's impact on modern policing is clearly felt through many of these contributions, as is Herman Goldstein's. But on the whole, the essays work together and reinforce the key tenets of community policing, with an emphasis on partnering with the community, using problem solving to address crime systematically, and transforming organizations (and their people) in ways that make the first two more effective.

Certain themes particularly intrigued us. For example, Michael Scott chose to grapple with the issue of measuring police effectiveness and raises the question: how can we plan for the future if we do not have an accurate measure of the extent of the problem? Others, including John Skinner and Joseph Brann, also raise the issue of the limitations of standard measures of crime and performance. The Uniform Crime Reports, while they continue to be the standard measure of crime (never quite replaced by the National Incident-Based Reporting System), remain fallible, but they are all we have at the moment. Maybe in these pages we see the beginning of a call to action to design a better system of measurement. Perhaps in 2022 we will see the national discourse focused on Scott's "index of leading public safety indicators" the same way that we currently talk about economic or public health indicators.

We also were interested to see that for many of the essayists, like Kriste Kibbey Etue and Harlin McEwen, technology is clearly a means to an end, and not the end itself. This is also true for the trio of essays written by Rick Fuentes, Jason Smith, and Jason O'Neal that are related to fusion centers and information sharing. In the recent era of rapid technological development, many of us clearly tend to latch on to the newest gadget as the solution to what ails us. After the shine wears off, its value is measured purely by how it enhances public safety. Technology cannot, and should not, replace good police work. Technology is a tool, but you have to learn how to use it, much like an old hammer, with focused precision lest you jam the nail right through to the other side or, worse yet, pound yourself on the thumb.

Technology cannot, and should not, replace good police work.

* * *

Another common theme concerns the people—not the public community, but the police community. Christopher Tracy, Charles Ramsey, and Edward Davis all speak to how the current climate offers both opportunities and challenges to ensuring that our nation's future police departments are staffed with well-trained, talented individuals and led by chiefs with clear, articulate visions. Many other essays make clear that leadership can occur at *any* level and that this idea will become only more important over the next decade. With the right recruitment tools, training programs, accountability systems, and collaboration between labor and management, agencies will be able to serve both their internal and external communities to the benefit of all.

Last, we chose to open this collection with the essays that focused on the "why" of it all. With more than 700,000 men and women going to work in law enforcement every day in this country, the philosophy behind what they do and why it matters cannot be overstated. Many of these contributors, like John Skinner, Louis Mayo, Ronald Glensor, Kenneth Peak, and J. Scott Thomson, all recognize that in many respects as much as things will change, some things will remain the same.

The desire to protect the soul of police work amidst the progress wrought by social, political, and economic changes, and the latest bandwagon, is evident. One thing that clearly shouldn't change by 2022 is that "policing always has been and will be about people," says Joseph Brann in his essay. From the first to the last essay—in which Chris Cognac sends us a letter from September 2022—every one of our contributors acknowledges that service to the community is at the heart of everything every police officer should do, both now and in the future. Keeping that principle at the forefront will ensure the legitimacy of police departments and the professionals who staff them.

What is the best way to read these essays? While we have grouped them into three areas around their primary focus—be that the motivation of the organization, the tools that make the job more productive, or the thin blue line itself—we don't believe there is a wrong order. Read this collection from front to back, from back to front, in alphabetical order, or by closing your eyes and pointing at a name in the table of contents to determine where to start.

We are confident this book will inspire you as much as it inspired us. Never have we been more proud to work for the COPS Office, in jobs that give us the opportunity to interact with the likes of these 27 contributors, and to help shape the public safety world of 2022. We'd like to take this perfect opportunity to thank some important people who made this book possible: Supervisory Analyst Robert Chapman, Assistant Director Matthew Scheider, and Deputy Director Sandra Webb for their support in allowing us the necessary time and resources; Amber Jabeen for helping us track RSVPs and get submission guidance out to all the correct people; and the creative and talented Erin P.T. Canning, Nancy Carlsen, and Fletcher Maffett of the COPS Office Publishing staff for a beautiful final product.

We were excited from the start of this project, and it never disappointed. For all who work in the policing field, you can take pride in the fact that your leaders are both thoughtful and creative. In his contribution, Tim Dolan talks about the "art of policing" coming from the "innate skills, smarts, experience, or traits that are inside a person [and] relates to a person's ability to interact, perceive, innovate, and act." If that is true, then this book is the collective wisdom of 27 artists. They not only are able to describe their vision for the future of public safety but also offer concrete ways on how to lead us there. Reading these essays has provided us with a sense of assurance that we are in good hands in the years to come. It also confirms there is work to be done and a shift in thought must take place if we are going to avail ourselves of the future promised to us in the pages that follow. Let's get started. ★

Section One

"...by 2022 chiefs may be able to answer accurately the all important question, 'What business are you in?'"

— Louis Mayo

★ ★ ★

The Future of Policing Can Be Found in the Past

by John P. Skinner

One of the most endearing images of American policing is that of the traditional foot patrol officer walking a beat and twirling a night stick. The image is powerful because it represents an era in policing when police officers were integrated into the fabric of the community they served. An effective foot patrol officer walked the beat, knew everyone in the neighborhood, and problem solved complex issues and problems.

The community identified the officer as one of its own and developed an informal network of communication based on collaborative partnerships and a mutual level of trust. Perhaps most important, the mere presence of the officer walking the beat often contributed to a sense of safety and security within the neighborhood.

> At its core, policing is about community service. It is about making neighborhoods stronger and fostering an unwavering feeling of safety and security.
>
> ⋆   ⋆   ⋆

Unfortunately, many positive aspects of this style of policing have been lost through the modernization of society and the evolution of technology. Over the last decade, it has become fashionable for departments to initiate community policing programs and cite industry buzzwords, only to discover later that the true foundation of policing can't be found in any single program; it must be embraced as a philosophical strategy.

In the pursuit of effectiveness and efficiency, many big city police departments have turned away from the core fundamentals of building community trust though interpersonal relations. The creation of the 911 emergency response system and the increased reliance of police vehicles have developed an entire new law enforcement system around rapid response and reaction. Within this system, police officers have lost their identity within the community. With little time to spend on interaction, relationship building, and problem solving, modern day police officers are less

of a partner with the neighborhoods they serve and more like a rapidly moving force, separated from the community by a high-speed cage of glass and steel.

Through the integration of new technology, police agencies have also placed increased emphasis on specializations. Most modern departments are now compartmentalized into individual units that specialize in a distinct type of police work. Gang units, narcotics task forces, warrant apprehension teams, and special investigation squads were all created to address a specific area of concern. Although there are advantages to this strategy, the unintended consequence is that it creates a further layer of separation from the community.

Within this movement of specialization, communities can no longer identify and connect with that single officer who understands the demographics and individual needs of the neighborhood. Instead, the community is forced to navigate through the bureaucracy of the department, often getting passed from one section to another. In return, these specialized officers no longer feel a community level of responsibility. Their success and effectiveness is tied directly to their specialization and not to the fundamental service of neighborhoods.

Modernization and technology have also had a significant impact in how police departments are evaluated. An agency's success is now directly related to a statistical evaluation of Uniformed Crime Reports. The invention of CompStat has reinforced this general notion and, to the credit of its architects, has helped achieve crime reductions in many communities.

However, despite the success of this system, it fails to account for important aspects of law enforcement: e.g., quality of service and a community's perception of fear and safety.

Despite national reductions in violent crime, the perception of crime and safety in many communities remains unchanged, and police departments struggle in a public relations arena to maintain a balance between people's perception of crime versus the reality. Residents no longer feel any level of attachment to the police officers working within their neighborhoods, and the gap between police officers and the people they serve is rapidly widening. The combination of all of these dynamics has brought policing in the United States to a critical crossroads.

The future success of American policing lies in the ability to recognize these important conditions and develop strategies that focus on redefining the relationship between police officers and the community. These strategies need to go well beyond implementing a single program or assigning a small group of officers to work on community-related affairs. The development of these strategies must address the rebirth of the fundamental philosophy of police-community partnership.

The foundation of this philosophy must be incorporated into all levels of training within police agencies. Interpersonal communication skills, problem solving techniques, and strategies to build positive community relationships must become the cornerstones of police training programs. New officers should be

> ## Despite national reductions in violent crime, the perception of crime and safety in many communities remains unchanged...

> * * *

indoctrinated in these programs during their time in the police academy, and then the programs should be continually reinforced during annual in-service sessions.

The increased availability of technology for police agencies is exciting and has created limitless possibilities. However, despite these possibilities, there needs to be a concerted effort to invest specifically in technology that promotes positive interaction and communication between the police and the public. Investments in mobile handheld communication devices would encourage officers to leave the confinement of their vehicles to interact with the community, while still allowing access to important information.

Most important, police departments must build new evaluation tools that go beyond the simple comparison of Uniformed Crime Report data. These new evaluation tools need to measure the community's assessment of quality of police service, the perception of crime, and the effectiveness of police strategies.

Specific emphasis needs to be placed on evaluating a police agency's response and support of crime victims. The success of any police department must become intertwined with the accessibility and satisfaction of the community it serves.

At its core, policing is about community service. It is about making neighborhoods stronger and fostering an unwavering feeling of safety and security. The police officers of the past who walked their foot patrols and spun their nightsticks understood this and embraced their important role within the community. The police officers of the future will be forced to navigate through a complex society and will be called upon to address new challenges. They will be drawn toward new technologies and encouraged to be more efficient. As these officers advance toward the future, it is imperative that they remember the past. ✳

John P. Skinner is the deputy police commissioner of the Baltimore (Maryland) Police Department. He is responsible for the day-to-day management and oversight of the agency's administrative operations. With 20 years of law enforcement experience, Skinner manages the department's $370 million budget and oversees the recruitment, hiring, training, planning, and information management of the nation's ninth largest police agency. Over the course of his career, Skinner has served in multiple investigative and patrol-related positions, including commanding officer of the Western and Central Districts, which encompass Baltimore's downtown and Inner Harbor areas. In 2008, he was appointed chief of the Patrol Division, where he commanded all of the agency's uniformed personnel. He has been recognized by the U.S. Department of Justice for developing the Baltimore Police Department's Patrol Response Survey, an evaluation program that measures the community's perception of police performance. He was also named the 2006 Baltimorean of the Year by Baltimore Magazine and was selected to represent the city of Baltimore at the 2,500th anniversary of the original marathon in Athens, Greece. Skinner holds a master's degree from the University of Baltimore and is an associate professor of criminal justice at Towson University in Maryland.

★ ★ ★

New Police Management Practices and Predictive Software: A New Era They Do Not Make

by Ronald W. Glensor
and Kenneth J. Peak

It is always interesting to read professional magazine and journal articles where the authors make bold predictions about policing's future based on a single program or strategy. Some of the predictions are tantamount to putting a powerful new engine and other upgrades into a 1960s' vintage Ford Mustang and then giving it a new name: does the modification or new technology improve the car's performance? Absolutely, but they do not change what the car is fundamentally—a vintage Mustang. Similarly, some people view the next era of policing as being intelligence-led or predictive policing. Still, others say we are in an information era or that "we're not doing community policing now, we're doing CompStat."

We believe that the general use—and at times misuse—of words such as "era" and police use of language and clichés are problematic and create more harm and confusion than they help.

If you wish to converse with me, define your terms.

–Voltaire

*   *   *

Furthermore, policing is indeed in an information "age" but not in an information "era." What have historically been touted by many as new eras of policing were in fact tactics and management tools, which remain an integral part of community policing and problem solving.

We hope this discussion serves as a case in point and the beginning of constructive discussions about the importance of language in policing. In examining the use of clichés in policing, first consider the views of Chris Braiden, former police superintendent in Edmonton, Canada:

> The problem with cliché policing is that it waters down the purpose. Over time, the purpose fades into the background as clichés proliferate. No need for clichés. The latest cliché? Intelligence-led policing, which says something itself about policing's past.[1]

Those police practitioners of considerable longevity can easily identify with Braiden's assessment and tendencies to re-label things—and they can probably add a few more labels of their own. The time has come to seriously question this use of clichés and tendency to label things anew. Why does this happen at all? After all, in most professions emphasis is placed on establishing foundations and then building on them, not replacing them.

This is not a minor issue for the field. Indeed, one of the long-standing, major criticisms of policing has been its tendency to quickly and, to some, blithely put new labels on different strategies and tactics (which have sometimes been caustically termed the "flavor of the month") and to use labels that are not altogether accurate. This criticism has certainly been lodged against community policing, owing to the fact that in the past some agencies failed to properly articulate, grasp, train for, and implement the strategy, too often creating a peripheral "unit" or, say, simply assigning an officer to bicycle or foot patrol and then anointing theirs a community policing organization. In a related vein, this lack of consistency of practice in problem solving has long been felt to frustrate—and even prevent—attempts to empirically evaluate efforts of community policing and problem solving.

What are intelligence-led policing and predictive policing, and why do some people wish to ascribe to them a new "era" in policing? Perhaps it would first be useful to consider what might constitute—or does not constitute—a new era in policing.

A review of the policing literature would lead most rational people to believe that nearly everything that has been launched anew constitutes an "era," as opposed to being a mere strategy. For example, for many the police-community relations era emerged from the political and social upheavals of the 1960s.

And the team policing era—which was formulated in the 1970s and sought to decentralize the delivery of police services and make police officers generalists—failed largely due to poor planning and implementation. Furthermore, street officers had no idea what they were supposed to be doing under this strategy, which was described as a new era.

More recently, the term "intelligence-led policing" originated in the late 1990s in Great Britain, where police believed that "a relatively small number of people were responsible for a comparatively large percentage of crimes" and that "police officers would have the best effect on crime by focusing on the most prevalent offenses occurring in their jurisdiction."[2] They also needed to manage law enforcement resources efficiently and to respond effectively to serious crime. In 2000, Britain's National Intelligence Criminal Service, which developed a National Intelligence Model, set priorities for the police service:[3]

- Target prolific offenders through overt and covert means.
- Manage crime and disorder hotspots.
- Identify and investigate linked series of crime or incidents.
- Apply a range of prevention measures such as closed-circuit television and lighting schemes or community action initiatives.

These priorities comprise problem solving—a part of problem-oriented policing—that is at the heart of the community era of policing. It is a management process placing greater emphasis than ever before on gathering information and performing higher levels of analyses.

> Policing simply cannot afford to continue debating acronyms, strategies, and eras as it proceeds into a future that promises a rapidly changing environment.

★ ★ ★

Many police agencies have the wherewithal to employ both crime analysts and intelligence analysts. Crime analysts keep their fingers on the pulse of crime in the jurisdiction: e.g., which crime trends are up, which are down, where the hot spots are, and what type of property is being stolen. Intelligence analysts, on the other hand, are likely to be more aware of the specific people and groups who are responsible for crime in the jurisdiction: e.g., who they are, where they live, what they do, and who they associate with. Unifying and utilizing both of these functions—crime analysis and intelligence analysis—is essential for obtaining a comprehensive grasp of the crime picture. In other words, crime analysis allows police to understand the what, when, and where while intelligence analysis allows police to understand who is involved, such as crime networks and individuals.[4]

Turning again to why succinct language is needed in policing, a ranking member of the Los Angeles Police Department once described predictive policing and intelligence-led policing as follows:

13

The LAPD has assumed a leadership role in translating these successes into the next era of policing: predictive policing. By developing, refining, and successfully executing on the predictive-policing model, the LAPD is leveraging the promise of advanced analytics in the prevention of and response to crime.

[Intelligence-led policing] does not replace the community involvement and problem-solving approaches in the community-policing model; it extends them to include research-based approaches, information and communications technology, and increased information sharing and accountability.[5]

With what we believe is a high degree of irony, a mere two months before the above comments were published, an assistant U.S. Attorney General stated that:

I think our first order of business is to define what we mean by "predictive policing." We've become so accustomed to labels in law enforcement. Is predictive policing just another label for another policing model? Or is it a larger concept—something that incorporates many policing paradigms?"[6]

These differing points of view concerning the work of policing is obviously confusing—and such blithe traversing from one description to another of policing can only serve to undercut the good work that police do. As indicated above, the police have long suffered under the yoke of the "flavor-of-the-month" criticism, and it is time to be much more wary in terms of describing its role and functions.

According to the report, *Navigating Your Agency's Path to Intelligence Led Policing*, intelligence-led policing "builds upon many of the tenets of the [Office of] Community Oriented Policing Services (COPS [Office]) program" and is defined as:

A collaborative law enforcement approach combining problem-solving policing, information sharing, and police accountability, with enhanced intelligence operations.

[Intelligence-led policing] is not a new policing model but, rather, an integrated enhancement that can contribute to public safety…whether it is community-oriented policing, problem-oriented policing, or other methodology.[7]

In sum, community oriented policing, problem solving, intelligence-led policing, and predictive policing are not separate and distinct entities and strategies. Rather, intelligence-led policing and predictive policing will advance the evolution of community oriented policing and problem solving to address 21st century challenges of crime and disorder. There is no compelling need to create a separate term or "era" that attempts to emphasize these two complements to policing. Policing simply cannot afford to continue debating acronyms, strategies, and eras as it proceeds into a future that promises a rapidly changing environment. ★

Ronald W. Glensor is a retired assistant chief of the Reno (Nevada) Police Department. He has more than 34 years of policing experience and has commanded the department's Patrol, Administration, and Detective divisions. Glensor is recognized internationally for his work in community policing and has provided assistance to more than 750 agencies throughout the United States, Canada, Australia, and Great Britain and has been a judge for the Herman Goldstein Awards since its inception. He is a consultant for the U.S. Department of Justice and Department of Homeland Security. In 1996, he was selected as one of only 10 U.S. public policy experts to receive an Atlantic Fellowship and traveled overseas to examine repeat victimization with the Home Office in London, England. His awards include the University of Nevada Alumni Association's Outstanding Achievement Award in 1996 and the Police Executive Research Forum's Gary P. Hayes Leadership Award in 1997. Glensor has co-authored *Community Policing and Problem Solving: Strategies and Practices*; *Police Supervision*; and *Policing Communities: Understanding Crime and Solving Problems*. He has a master's degree in public administration and policy and a doctorate in political science from the University of Nevada.

Kenneth J. Peak is a full professor and past chairman of the Department of Criminal Justice at the University of Nevada, Reno. He entered municipal policing in Pittsburg, Kansas, in 1970 and subsequently held positions as a nine-county criminal justice planner for southeast Kansas, director of a four-state Technical Assistance Institute for the federal Law Enforcement Assistance Administration, director of university police at Pittsburg State University and the University of Nevada, Reno, and assistant professor of criminal justice at Wichita State University. He has authored or co-authored 25 textbooks focusing on a variety of policing and justice administration subjects, two historical books (on Midwestern bootlegging and temperance), and nearly 60 monographs, journal articles, and invited chapters.

Endnotes

1. Braiden, Chris, "Cliché Policing: Answer Before Question" (unpublished paper).

2. Peterson, Marilyn. *Intelligence-Led Policing: The New Intelligence Architecture* (Washington, D.C.: U.S. Department of Justice, Bureau of Justice Assistance, 2005), 9, www.ncjrs.gov/pdffiles1/bja/210681.pdf.

3. The *National Intelligence Model* (London: National Criminal Intelligence Service, 2000), www.intelligenceanalysis.net/National%20Intelligence%20Model.pdf.

4. Bruce, Christopher, quotation in *Integrated Intelligence and Crime Analysis: Enhanced Information Management for Law Enforcement Leaders,* by J. H. Ratcliffe (Washington, D.C.: Police Foundation, 2007), 16, www.cops.usdoj.gov/Publications/integratedanalysis.pdf.

5. Beck, Charlie. "Predictive Policing: What Can We Learn from Wal-Mart and Amazon about Fighting Crime in a Recession?" *The Police Chief* 76, no. 11 (November 2009), 18–24.

6. Robinson, Laurie, "Predictive Policing Symposium: Opening Remarks" (speech given at the Predictive Policing Symposium in Los Angeles, California, November 18, 2009), www.nij.gov/topics/law-enforcement/strategies/predictive-policing/symposium/opening-robinson.htm.

7. Global Justice Information Sharing Initiative, *Navigating Your Agency's Path to Intelligence-Led Policing* (Washington, D.C.: U.S. Department of Justice, Bureau of Justice Assistance, 2009), www.it.ojp.gov/gist/Document/38.

★ ★ ★

Preparing the Police for an Uncertain Future: Four Guiding Principles

by Jim Bueermann

One of the more arduous challenges police leaders face is preparing their organizations for an increasingly hard-to-predict future. The last decade has demonstrated just how difficult it is to forecast social, technological, economic, and political trends and events, which can impact public safety and result in calls for police action.

Broadly, police responses are typically grounded in either guiding principles or tradition and organizational culture. The latter does not necessarily guarantee effective outcomes but may be more comfortable for some than reframing organizational paradigms.

Policing's future is fraught with uncertainty; therefore, it needs a set of coherent, organizational development principles that prepare police officers to manage their evolving world, regardless of its future state. These principles must reflect American democratic ideals.

Historically, police departments have done much better in training their officers on the technical aspects of the job than in preparing them for evolving futures.

* * *

They need to mirror the public mandate for responsive, equitable policing. These principles must also be anchored to the culture of American policing, and they must be flexible enough to ride the unpredictable waves of change.

The four guiding principles presented here are predicated on those articulated by Sir Robert Peel in the 1800s. They represent a framework for helping the police to think expansively about their future—no matter what it is—and their relationship with the people whom they serve.

Historically, police departments have done much better in training their officers on the technical aspects of the job than in preparing them for evolving futures. Investigative or procedural techniques are much more likely to be part of police training curricula than the theoretical underpinnings of cultural literacy, police legitimacy, or evidence-based policing. While an increasing number of thoughtful police leaders are introducing their personnel to these forward-thinking ideas, the majority of organizational development in police departments is framed around slow, incremental change. This would be reasonable if the world was evolving at a slow, incremental pace, but, as we know, that is not the case.

Police leaders are obligated to help their followers understand not just "what" to think, but "how" to think about the world ahead of them. And the "how" may be radically different from the way contemporary leaders themselves were taught to think about policing. The following principles will help leaders effect meaningful, future-oriented organizational change.

Principle 1: Be value-driven

When police departments establish a set of organizational values—especially when they do so with community input—they create a foundational belief system on which all organizational and individual decision making can be based. For instance, articulating that collaboration, leadership, ethics, excellence, and the respect for human dignity are an organization's core values means that everything within it—from recruitment, promotions, and discipline to training in police legitimacy and procedural justice—must be in alignment with what the organization purports to believe. In the future, effective police departments will align everything they do with democratically framed values reflecting their community commitment.

Principle 2: Be a catalyst for change

The recession has demonstrated that the police can't afford to control crime and disorder all by themselves. And they can't do this by employing outdated practices perpetuated by tradition, rather than by being motivated by desired outcomes. In the future, police departments will act as brokers, rather than providers, of many crime control products and services. Increasingly, they will define their role as a catalyst and facilitator of community action by defining crime and disorder problems and then interweaving scarce public and private resources to solve those problems that do not mandate substantial police intervention.

Victim services, drug court interventions, prisoner reentry programs, and focused deterrence programs aimed at curbing the behavior of known offenders are examples of important crime control strategies that lend themselves to police leadership without the use of extensive police resources. When the police serve as a catalyst for change, they are more likely to manage desired changes, rather than be managed by the forces of change.

The role of what is essentially a crime control social activist may be uncomfortable for many police departments. However, leadership, by definition, requires appropriate risk-taking, a tolerance for ambiguity, and courage. If police departments are to control their own destinies, they must lead change—not be subject to it. This includes internal organizational changes along with external changes in the community. Assuming the role of a community change agent requires a clearly articulated set of organizational values and the intestinal fortitude that is the hallmark of true leadership.

> …police departments must become learning organizations, capable of experimenting, evaluating, and modifying their approaches…

* * *

Principle 3: Be legitimate to those whom you serve

News reports are replete with police departments that have become disconnected from the communities they serve. Claims of biased-based policing and inappropriate use of force are seemingly commonplace. Growing is the number of incidents of wrongful conviction in which police behavior is questionable.

When people perceive the police as legitimate in their actions, they are more likely to comply with police orders and obey the law. They are more likely to cooperate with officers; and, as a result, both the police and citizens are safer.

On an interpersonal level, police legitimacy requires the police to be fair, neutral, and unbiased in their decision making. It also requires they treat people with courtesy, dignity, and respect. At an organizational level, the manner in which police officers feel they

> In the future, police departments…will define their role as a catalyst and facilitator of community action…

* * *

are treated by the leadership of the department creates a sense of internal police legitimacy and frames officer–citizen interactions. And from a community perspective, police legitimacy requires police departments to act in a manner consistent with the adage of "investing in the bank of community trust"—because they will make a withdrawal at some point (e.g., community reaction to police use of force).

The essence of police legitimacy is straightforward. Community safety is enhanced when (1) police departments articulate a core set of values framed around the theoretical underpinnings of police legitimacy, (2) they lead change within themselves as well as in the community, and (3) they train and hold police officers accountable for behaving in highly legitimate ways.

Principle 4: Be a learning organization

Fortune 500 companies count intellectual capital among their most valuable assets. They all have some form of a knowledge management initiative to leverage what their employees know about their products, services, customers, and operating environments. Similarly, successful police departments in the future will find themselves actively managing the crime and disorder knowledge of their officers, justice system partners, and community members. The extent to which departments capture, use, share, and increase what they know about crime and disorder will largely determine their future success.

Inherent in any effective effort to manage knowledge is the notion of on-going learning and evaluation. Successful private sector organizations constantly review the best evidence of what works in their markets, develop strategies based on that evidence, and then evaluate them for success. In other words, they constantly experiment with ways to improve their profits and learn from those experiences. In policing, the equivalent of this is known as evidence-based policing. It is a thoughtful approach to using the best available evidence about what works to control crime to drive policing strategy and is a gateway concept to police departments becoming "learning organizations."

In the coming years, police resources are likely to become even more constrained. As a result, it will be crucial that police departments experiment with ways to improve their bottom line of community safety and employ smart policing strategies based on the best available evidence. Like the private sector, the police will need to commit to evidence-based practices—either developed by researchers or themselves—to enhance the safety of their communities.

To accomplish diverse community safety goals, police departments must become learning organizations, capable of experimenting, evaluating, and modifying their approaches as a result of those evaluations. Moreover, they will have to do this within a framework that aligns activities with clear organizational values, furthers their role as catalysts of community action, enhances the public's perception of their legitimacy, and uses evidence to drive police practices.

In the future, the police will have to think differently about their relationship with their community, their role in society, and the manner in which they craft responses to crime. Police leaders will have to sharpen their focus on preparing their organizations for volatile, uncertain futures. With this in mind, we can apply to the control of crime and disorder Albert Einstein's view that "the world we created today…has problems which cannot be solved by thinking the way we thought when we created them." By acting in accordance with the guiding principles laid out here, police leaders can effectively prepare their organizations to better serve the public now and in the future. ★

Jim Bueermann, president of the Police Foundation, worked for the Redlands (California) Police Department for 33 years, serving in every unit within the department. He was appointed chief of police and director of Housing, Recreation, and Senior Services in 1998 and served in that role until his retirement in June of 2011. He then served as an executive fellow with the U.S. Department of Justice's National Institute of Justice and a senior fellow at George Mason University. An honorary fellow of the Academy of Experimental Criminology, Bueerman has also been elected into the halls of fame at George Mason University's Center for Evidence-Based Crime Policy and the College of Social and Behavioral Sciences at California State University, San Bernardino. He is a graduate of California State University, San Bernardino, the University of Redlands, the FBI National Academy, and the California Command College.

★ ★ ★

Quality and Performance Management: An Innovative Approach to Future Police Management

by Michael T. Frazier

Law enforcement executives all over the world are traditionally tasked with similar missions, including:

- Suppressing crime

- Collaborating with the community to determine service expectations

- Working closely with all levels of local, county, state, and federal governments

- Aligning available law enforcement resources to determine and meet all safety and security expectations effectively and efficiently

While those mission objectives are not likely to change over the next 10 years, successful law enforcement agencies will expand the expertise of their personnel in the use of proven business management principles and techniques that will complement their crime-fighting, leadership, and communication capabilities.

Adding these business tools will assist agencies in not only providing effective safety and security services but also providing them through a management capability that will rival successful businesses all over the world.

As a major drain of any city budget, the law enforcement agency will operate more efficiently to ensure the equitable distribution of limited public funds. Through the development of a solid law enforcement business management culture, those mission objectives identified above will be reached effectively by the expanded commitment to manage the agency as a business system comprised of interrelated working parts, namely:

- **Planning and performance management:** Planning for short-, mid-, and long-term objectives to ensure an aligned focus, identified success factors, regular performance reviews, and enhanced organizational performance

- **Resource management:** Identifying, providing, and efficiently managing the provision of resources, including hiring, facilities, equipment, financial, and information

- **Core product/service management:** Identifying, measuring, challenging, and continually improving the core competencies of the agency, including patrol, investigations, and all support services

- **Measurement, analysis, and improvement:** Ensuring that customer input is valued and sought after and service levels are regularly satisfied, including performance evaluation and improvement, service consistency, internal performance auditing beyond compliance audits, and corrective action techniques that ultimately repair problem root causes to eliminate reoccurrence

- **Knowledge/quality management:** Creating an environment that fosters individual and organizational learning and growth, ensures continuity, and relieves challenges related to succession planning

The management model that will be used to transition agencies to a state of law enforcement business excellence will be based on a complementary relationship of compliance with generally accepted national and/or state accreditation standards and international business management standards, currently managed by the International Organization of Standardization. Through this complementary relationship, the law enforcement agency will have added considerable value to its accreditation process, streamlined the compliance/maintenance processes, enabled and encouraged the development of relevant performance metrics beyond traditional law enforcement measurements, and effectively responded to recent economic challenges. This effective balance between law enforcement compliance and business performance will continue to elevate each agency's relationship with the community it serves.

Surprise Police Department's ISO quality management system model is a connected system of interrelated parts.

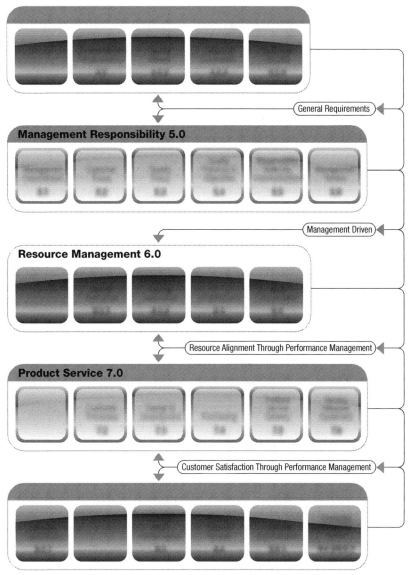

Source: Copyright 2011 Surprise (Arizona) Police Department.

> The law enforcement agency that commits to learning and applying effective business management principles and performs as a component system is better equipped to succeed in all areas of law enforcement responsibility.

* * *

The guiding principles that will shape the future of law enforcement management are expected to evolve as do internationally accepted business management principles. The basis for these principles, however, will likely remain steadfast as a set of fundamental beliefs that are essential for leading and operating a law enforcement agency "aimed at continually improving performance over the long term by focusing on customers while addressing the needs of all other interested parties."[1] The following principles will be used throughout the organization to enhance the management system components identified above:[2]

- **Customer focus:** "Organizations depend on their customers and therefore should understand current and future customer needs, should meet customer requirements, and strive to exceed customer expectations."

Organizations focusing on their customers will likely increase operational effectiveness and efficiency and enhance trust, credibility, and reputation.

- **Leadership:** "Leaders establish unity of purpose and direction of the organization. They should create and maintain the internal environment in which people can become fully involved in achieving the organization's objectives."

Effective law enforcement leaders applying this principle will elevate information consistency, promote alignment and understanding of departmental processes and objectives, communicate the value of accreditation and management standards, and reduce probability for miscommunication.

- **Involvement of people:** "People at all levels are the essence of an organization, and their full involvement enables their abilities to be used for the organization's benefit."

Employee involvement typically results in an organization comprised of motivated people who are eager to contribute, people who are willing to participate, people who are willing to be held accountable for the development of individual and organizational objectives and performance related to those objectives, and people who are willing to participate in change and continual improvement.

- **Process approach:** "A desired result is achieved more efficiently when activities and related resources are managed as a process."

Effectively developing and managing required, efficient processes will reduce redundancy, eliminate waste, reduce cost through control and elimination of corrective action needs, establish predictability of results, promote efficiency through effective use of limited resources, and prioritize opportunities for improvement.

- **System approach to management:** "Identifying, understanding, and managing interrelated processes as a system contributes to the organization's effectiveness and efficiency in achieving its objectives."

An organization performs through a unified approach of all parties. The system approach will reduce individual agendas and inequitable allocations of resources and will promote consistency in objective development. The organization will then become more efficient, more effective, and a better place to work.

- **Continual improvement:** "Continual improvement of the organization's overall performance should be a permanent objective of the organization."

All members of the organization should continually examine performance and look for better ways of doing business and strengthening alignment. Similarly, the organization should regularly examine its products and services to ensure they still meet customer needs, are technologically current or advanced, are in compliance with standards, and are in alignment with current regulatory and statutory requirements.

> [The] balance between law enforcement compliance and business performance will continue to elevate each agency's relationship with the community it serves.

* * *

- **Factual approach to decision-making:** "Effective decisions are based on the analysis of data and information."

Organizations can improve only what is being measured. Decision making will be better supported with objective information rather than subjective reactions. Balancing factual information with experience, knowledge, and opinions will assist in selecting the best of competing ideas.

- **Mutually beneficial supplier relationships:** "An organization and its suppliers are interdependent, and a mutually beneficial relationship enhances the ability of both to create value."

Similar to the organization's reliance on customers to enable it to continue operating as a vital public safety entity, the agency must also have a solid relationship with its suppliers to ensure they understand the organization's needs as they ultimately relate to providing services to its customers.[3]

Several law enforcement agencies throughout Europe and Asia have applied this business methodology for several years. However, only a few agencies in the United States—including in Houston, Texas; Phoenix, Arizona; Clark County School District, Nevada; and Surprise, Arizona—have become considerably more effective and efficient by formally adopting and successfully implementing the business philosophy.

The law enforcement agency that commits to learning and applying effective business management principles and performs as a component system is better equipped to succeed in all areas of law enforcement responsibility. The agency will be more focused on its customers, be more connected internally to ensure consistency and efficiency, and possess a management capability to evaluate and respond positively to performance data beyond customary clearance rates, crime rates, and response times—all in an effort to develop a world-class business that just happens to provide safety and security services that consistently meet community needs at the level expected. ✫

Michael T. Frazier

was appointed as the chief of police for the city of Surprise, Arizona, on February 14, 2011. Previously, Frazier served as the chief for the city of El Mirage, Arizona, for just over three years. As chief, he is responsible for all aspects of the police department in serving the needs of the community. This responsibility, as it was in El Mirage, is characterized by a changing culture and a heightened professionalism within the organization. Focusing on community policing, developing protocols and effective business practices, and building a solid foundation for providing effective customer service are dramatically changing the way the department is perceived by the community. Frazier began his law enforcement career with the Phoenix (Arizona) Police Department, serving in nearly every division for 32 years until retiring in October 2007. While with Phoenix, Frazier rose through the ranks, retiring as the executive assistant chief of police. In that role, he was responsible for a $600 million budget and the day-to-day operations of the department, including patrol, investigations, and tactical operations. Frazier holds a bachelor's degree in justice studies from Arizona State University and master's degree in educational leadership from Northern Arizona University.

Endnotes

1. Hoyle, David. *ISO 9000 Quality System Handbook* (London: Butterworth-Heinemann, 2006).

2. The eight listed principles and quotations are from the International Organization for Standardization. *Quality Management Principles* (Genève, Switzerland: ISO Central Secretariat, 2011). www.iso.org/iso/qmp_2012.pdf.

3. Amari, David M., "Creating a Police Quality Management System—How the Surprise Police Department Combines CALEA Accreditation and ISO 9001:2008 Quality Management Principles." *CALEA Update Magazine* 108 (February 2012).

★ ★ ★

Community Building as Crime Control

by Michael A. Davis

What fundamentally separates police from the rest of society is the authority to utilize corrosive force. Police have almost exclusive rights to exercise formal control in areas of crime and disorder. Historically, through the eras of policing (political, reform, and community) in the United States, the police have focused their innovations in the area of how to levy force in a more fair, impartial, and thus more effective way.

What has remained constant in policing is the fundamental belief that public safety is achieved only through exercising formal control. Some police chiefs, I'm sure, would quibble with this assertion, touting what they believe are broad, holistic efforts at reducing crime. The problem is that, despite the best intentions, it is rare to find police officers working the street who see their role extending much beyond that of an instrument of formal control.

> ...our charge is not to simply be reflexive to crime trends but to challenge those conditions that contribute to crime and disorder.

*　*　*

This misguided ethos of patrol officers was illustrated in a recent article[1] that focused pejoratively on what the author described as hug-a-thug initiatives promulgated by police administrators. The illustrations accompanying this article featured minority males dressed in urban fashion in emotionally charged situations. The author insinuated that any outreach effort was akin to extending a capitulating hand across enemy lines and proclaimed that "what warriors do best is keep the damned in check."

I present this example not to say that all patrol officers have malevolent intent but that the culture perpetuated through generations of myopic police leadership has led to this unhelpful mentality of patrol officers. In fact, there is significant research that enforcement-only crime reduction measures have led to decreased policing legitimacy and thus decreased effectiveness in the communities that need the police the most.

It would be inaccurate to state that policing has not evolved some in the last three decades, but the question is have we done more harm than good under the fundamental principles of community policing, which stress more than anything else improving the conditions of the communities we serve? This is a topic where there is an easy fight to pick, especially with those law and order purists who quickly point to 30-year lows in crime across the United States and give almost all the credit to high-intensity law enforcement.

The correlation between full jails and low crime falls right into the police ethos of law and order that seems to have a high tolerance for collateral damage in poor (and minority) communities. Sure, crime is down. But for some communities crime has never gone down (significantly), and in some cities violent crime is making a comeback. So, if disadvantaged neighborhoods are still fertile ground for crime, then this crime dip is ephemeral.

My assertion is that the police over the past couple of decades have done little to change the conditions in communities that allow crime to exist. In fact, if one were to believe that the effects of mass incarceration reduce a community's capacity to prevent crime, then police have done more harm than good in some communities of color.

As police, I believe our charge is not to simply be reflexive to crime trends and patterns but to challenge those conditions that contribute to crime and disorder. This approach requires more than working with the community (as purported by community policing) but actually being part of the community, creating an intended future that is distinct from the past. I call this approach asset-based, police-led community building. This policing philosophy is focused on the gifts and assets of a community and treats crime as a symptom of disconnected community. One of the goals of this policing strategy is building active social capital throughout the community. When we activate community members to lay claim to this place and the people within it, we reverse the pathology of the isolation and dependency that cripples a community's ability to prevent crime.

Asset-based community policing's implementation is evolutionary, not revolutionary. This approach requires layers of strategies that engage and activate more and more people in each initiative. The accumulative effect of the complete orientation of police services to building active social capital will challenge those conditions that lead to crime.

So, where to begin is the age-old question. I believe that a shift in focus and a shift in behaviors will begin the process. Community building cannot be viewed as the secondary but primary objective of police departments. The police have to play a lead role in this process because community members will take the path of least resistance and demand everything from the police and expect nothing from themselves in creating a safer place.

To begin the process of community building, the police can do three things:

1. **Work to build a culturally competent community:** People who live in diverse communities fear demographic change, and that fear leads efforts to leverage the police to mitigate that fear. Building a competent community creates a working trust between communities of color and the

> ## Patrol officers are a police department's greatest source of ideas and…strategies for this community-building approach to policing.

*　*　*

dominate race and removes the police from the middle. This focus would by default raise the level of police legitimacy in diverse communities. This means police departments need to focus on connecting residents to one another, creating the space for conversations focused on gifts, assets, and the common future we can build for this place we call our community.

2. **Stop letting residents off the hook:** Generally, residents don't care much about crime until it impacts them. Residents view themselves as consumers of services without any responsibility to serve one another to build a collective future. By enhancing the level of collective efficacy in a community, the muscle of informal social control would strengthen, thereby reducing dependency on the police for every issue requiring a control remedy. This means changing the conversation from a transactional and deficit focus to an asset-based focus on relationships. This would not only raise the level of police legitimacy but also curb the incessant need to add cops to the payroll.

3. **Get patrol officers to focus on community-building outcomes:** Police organizations have orientated patrol officers as a group to focus almost exclusively in arcane enforcement-only crime control tasks. Police departments don't promote, measure, or reward (and thereby don't value) community-building policing approaches. Because of this failure in leadership, patrol officers are stuck in a perpetual cycle of low-reward and high-stress enforcement-only strategies. Changing this dynamic begins by the alignment of awards and accountability systems to the advancement of collective efficacy and the inculcation of the commensurate behaviors to geographic policing strategies. Officers who are orientated to care about outcomes will behave and make decisions according to how they will impact the whole and not simply whether or not they will violate policy. Patrol officers are a police department's greatest source of ideas and commensurate strategies for this community-building approach to policing. It's high time that police leaders engage these resources as the assets they are.

For police to be relevant and effective in the next 10 years, our approach of symptom-based, enforcement-based tactics must morph to a more sustainable and effective model. By leveraging the assets of the community, we can begin to create an intended future for our communities where the outcomes are more significant and conditions that lead to crime have been changed. ✭

Michael A. Davis has been in law enforcement for 20 years and has served as the chief of police for the city of Brooklyn Park, Minnesota, for over four years. Prior to joining the Brooklyn Park Police Department, Davis worked for the Minneapolis Police Department and served in such roles as the commander of the Internal Affairs Unit and sector lieutenant. Davis holds a master's degree in organizational management and a bachelor's degree in criminal justice. Davis is a member of the International Association of Chiefs of Police and the Police Executive Research Forum. He is also a member of the current Executive Session on Policing and Public Safety at the Harvard Kennedy School, John F. Kennedy School of Government. In April 2012, Davis was presented with the Gary P. Hayes Award for leadership and innovation from the Police Executive Research Forum.

Endnotes

1. Goetz. Ti. "Have You Hugged Your Thug Today." *American COP* 8. no. 1 (January/February 2012). http://fmgpublications.ipaperus.com/FMGPublications/AmericanCop/ACJF12/?Page=34.

★ ★ ★

Moving Beyond the Myths and Misdirection Impeding Community Policing Success

by Louis A. Mayo

All of local policing is impeded by a schizophrenic existence of confusion and conflict between the many myths and misdirection of policing, resulting in a fragile house of cards (myths) on a foundation of sand (misdirection). This is well clarified in the classic essay "Florence Nightingale in Pursuit of Willie Sutton,"[1] which describes local policing as more like the service orientation of Florence Nightingale than the law enforcement role of chasing criminals. Extensive research has quantified the local police role, indicating that rarely is an officer involved in "crime." In fact, my research indicates that the average police officer is involved in only one such crime incident per week—and that is usually to take a routine report about some prior property crime.

Why is U.S. policing called "law enforcement" since law enforcement is such a small part of policing?

* * *

The basic principle of community policing has been well known since 1829 when enunciated by Sir Robert Peel in his founding of the London police department and is equally true today. American policing is derived from the London model, but unfortunately this aspect/principle has been over-ridden by local culture. Of Peel's nine principles, two are key: the "police must secure the willing cooperation of the public…," and "the basic mission for which the police exist is to prevent crime and disorder."

After I once spoke at an FBI international symposium on policing, I was approached by two Australian police officials with puzzled looks on their faces. They asked, "Why is U.S. policing called 'law enforcement' since law enforcement is such a small part of policing?" The Australians are correct. The term law enforcement is a gross misnomer and distortion when referring to community, or any other, policing.

In 1967, the President's Crime Commission indicated that most police work does not involve crime,[2] and my research quantified it. Such gross misperception of the problem was articulated when I spoke at

a workshop to senior police officials and asked their estimate of how many major crime calls are answered per week by an average officer. Their replies were usually in the range of 15 to 25 calls per week. They looked on in doubtful amazement when told that research says the correct answer for almost all cities is one. They were then given a simple formula to compute the rate for their department and looked up in amazement when faced with the actual results.

With such gross misperceptions of an organization's activities, no chief executive can make good decisions for leadership. The world-famous management consultant Peter Drucker, when consulting with a new organization, frequently would ask what business are you in? The answer is not obvious. In the 1990s, John F. Smith, then-president of General Motors, astutely stated in a television interview that GM was actually in the entertainment industry. If their new cars were not emotionally exciting or entertaining, low sales would result in their bankruptcy.

So, what business are you in?

A common motto of policing is "to serve and protect." Throughout history, this has been to serve and protect the powerful from the powerless, a point made by Samuel Walker in his text, *Popular Justice*. Successful implementation of community policing must recognize the dramatic social and political implications of empowering the powerless from the police if the community of people are to see the police as friends and supporters and not hostile adversaries. All of the mechanics of community policing are really only methodology to that end.

In *Community Policing: The Past, Present and Future*,[3] the results of three national surveys of about 300 police departments reporting implementation of community policing are presented. However, none reported implementation of all of the community oriented policing elements and, according to Gary Cordner, "police agencies [tended] to adopt a relatively modest version of community policing" and "officers [seemed] to spend relatively little time actually engaging citizens."[4] Because community policing is a holistic philosophy, partial implementation will result in ineffective results, particularly because such departments combine traditional with community policing and these do not mix any more than oil and water. In that same text, Herman Goldstein stated "the initiatives associated with community policing cannot survive in a police agency managed in traditional ways,"[5] which are in direct conflict with the stated community policing principles of Peel.

Finally, a basic element of community policing is integrity, without which all the other principles and procedures are void. Police must not only act with complete integrity but also be perceived as such by the community. Unfortunately, as Lord Acton in England stated, "power tends to corrupt, and absolute power corrupts absolutely."[6] To see the risks of this in policing, we just have to look at the research of psychologist Philip Zimbardo in his famous experiment at Stanford University where he empowered some students to act as guards and others as prisoners, but he had to cancel the project when he found the guards abusing their power.

Despite this risk, in my over 60 years in policing, I have known only two chiefs with adequate corruption-prevention programs. That explains why the U.S. Department of Justice has found more than 30 departments guilty of patterns and practice (not isolated events) of civil rights abuse.[7] Yet many chiefs would not fire an officer for making a false official statement, even though it normally involves at least two felonies—perjury and obstruction of justice. Chiefs must understand the need for strong anti-corruption programs if community policing (or any policing) is to succeed.

Recognizing and correcting the many policing myths are critical to successful implementation of community policing, by first cleansing students' minds of the many policing myths and then recognizing that traditional and community policing do not mix, like oil and water. This is emphasized in the graduate curriculum in community policing, designed by myself and Dr. Diana Bruns at Southeast Missouri State University, which starts with cleansing students' minds of policing myths to help them accept the true/proven principles of community policing. Ultimate success has police and citizens' minds harmonized in cooperative unison versus opposed adversaries. If we work now to address these myths and misdirection across the board in our training and education programs, by 2022 chiefs may be able to answer accurately the all important question, "What business are you in?" ★

Louis A. Mayo has been engaged in advancing policing nationwide through research, operations, training, and management consulting since 1967. He is president of Mayo, Mayo and Associates, Inc., which is devoted to solving police management and operations problems. He is also the founder of the Police Association for College Education, a non-profit devoted to improving policing by advocating that all officers have at least a four-year college education, as recommended by national commissions and the federal courts. As staff co-founder of the National Institute of Justice, Mayo directed nationwide training programs to improve policing and other aspects of criminal justice, including courts, prosecution, and corrections. His service on a national committee to recommend training in police use of force resulted in a curriculum used to train many police agencies. Mayo also served as an associate member of the Federal Council for Science and Technology, the national science policy advisory board to the president. He was given the annual award "for outstanding national contribution to the advancement and professional development of criminal justice administration" by the criminal justice section of the American Society for Public Administration. Mayo developed the curriculum for the FBI National Academy on implementing police research, and he has been an invited speaker at the FBI academy on several occasions, including the International Symposium on the Future of Law Enforcement. His doctoral dissertation, "Analysis of the Role of the Police Chief Executive," was the first comprehensive analysis of this role in the United States.

Endnotes

1. Bittner, Egon. "Florence Nightingale in Pursuit of Willie Sutton: A Theory of Police." in *The Potential for Reform of Criminal Justice*, ed. H. Jacob (Beverly Hills, CA: Sage Publications, 1974), 17–34.

2. Task Force on the Police, *Task Force Reports: The Police* (Washington, D.C.: The President's Commission on Law Enforcement and Administration of Justice, 1967).

3. Fridell, Lorie, and Mary Ann Wycoff. eds., Community Policing: The Past, Present, and Future, (Washington, D.C.: Police Executive Research Forum, 2004), 65, www.policeforum.org/library/community-policing/CommunityPolicingReduced.pdf.

4. Ibid.

5. Goldstein, Herman. *The New Policing: Confronting Complexity,* NIJ Research in Brief (Washington, D.C.: U.S. Department of Justice, National Institute of Justice, 1993), quoted in *Community Policing: The Past, Present, and Future,* eds. Lorie Fridell and Mary Ann Wycoff (Washington, D.C.: Police Executive Research Forum, 2004), 8.

6. John Emerich Edward Dalberg Acton, First Baron Acton of Aldenham, was a 19th century British politician and historian. Considered one of the most learned men of his time and a vocal advocate of both religious and personal freedom, he is now best known for his often misquoted statement on the corruption of power.

★ ★ ★

Asking the Tough Questions

by Joseph Brann

Over the past two decades, most regions of the United States have experienced significant declines in the Part I crime rate, both in the violent and property crime categories. Although this long-term trend has been quite remarkable and unprecedented, it remains something the general public is largely unaware of and most often surprised by when it is pointed out to them. The media have not brought a great deal of attention to this, as they tend to focus on sensational crime stories and usually focus on crime data only when annual Uniform Crime Reports are released. Most police agencies and local officials routinely neglect to publicize long-term trends or fail to even recognize what has taken place in their own jurisdictions beyond looking at the seasonal or annual data. Even researchers and academics have difficulty explaining the reasons for this apparent but long-term reversal in crime.

Are we effective? Are we accountable? Are the results that we are seeking what the community expects?

* * *

Despite the progress in lowering crime over the long-term, we continue to witness increasing pressures on police organizations to achieve even better results. That includes seeking reductions in both crime and the fear of crime, improved cost-efficiency in the delivery of police services, heightened accountability for results at both the organizational level as well as on the part of all employees, and improved responsiveness to community and neighborhood issues/concerns. These pressures are likely going to increase even more in the future, and that is one of the challenges that must be met by the next generation of police leaders.

Some argue that these increasing demands and lofty goals are simply unattainable in light of the long-term reductions we have already experienced. Yet this crime reduction trend has continued even in an era of shrinking resources and a significant decline in the economy. There are lessons to be learned and opportunities before us if we choose to recognize some of the significant influences that have been at work. We can build upon the foundation that has been evolving for the past several decades and do even more if we so choose.

There is potential for even greater success if leaders, at all levels of police organizations, as well as elected policy-makers recognize that we cannot afford to be limited by past assumptions and myths that still haunt and limit the profession. Examples include thinking that the police can do little to prevent crime other than through increased enforcement and arrests, that crime rates are somehow tied to police staffing levels (especially that of sworn officers), that the public should do little more than act as the eyes and ears of the police, and that suppression and enforcement strategies are more effective than prevention strategies or multi-disciplinary approaches.

The roots and influence of many of the innovative policing strategies that began to proliferate in the 1990s, which is when we first began to witness widespread crime reductions across the country, were actually sown in the 1970s and 1980s. Police strategies shifted from being largely reactive in nature to exploring new methods for preventing both property crime (through such things as target hardening, crime prevention through environmental design, loss prevention techniques, etc.) and violent crime (improved public awareness through community education and training, sexual assault prevention, risk awareness and avoidance, etc.). Improved data mining capabilities evolved with the development of computer-aided dispatch/records management systems, and this opened the door to the emphasis on problem-solving tactics that focused on reducing repeat crimes and chronic nuisances associated with specific locations, offenders, and victims.

Those jurisdictions that were on the forefront of adopting these strategies, programs, and tactics were also the first to begin experiencing significant and lasting declines in their crime rates. Their successes preceded the national trend and prompted other communities to examine what was happening and to adopt similar approaches.

While the police have most certainly played a role in reducing crime, it would be foolhardy to not recognize that a number of factors have influenced this trend, including the fact that even the nature of crime has been changing. In the past, most policing strategies have largely focused on Part I crimes. The effectiveness of policing strategies, responses from our criminal justice system, and shifts in crime policies along with shifts in demographics have all contributed to some subtle but significant changes in criminal behavior and victimization.

There is a decided shift taking place in the types of crimes being committed today, with a pronounced increase found in the Part II crime category; more crime has become evident in areas related to identity theft, fraud, white collar crime, and other categories that do not necessarily get the attention of the media when they focus on crime data. And most members of the public do not understand the difference between Part I and Part II crimes. Additionally, significant police resources are rarely committed to Part II crimes, other than for drug and vice offenses.

This decline in Part I crimes and shift toward Part II crimes warrant a closer examination to ascertain whether other factors could be at work and whether

police strategies and resources are being adjusted to ensure the public's needs are being met. Is the current crime decline actually the result of improvements in policing strategies and crime policies, or might it reflect a failure on the part of the police to recognize that shifts are occurring in criminal behavior because offenders realize that Part II crimes receive less attention from police and prosecutors? If so, does this reflect awareness on the part of career criminals that the likelihood of getting caught for these crimes is considerably less and that, even if apprehended, the sanctions are virtually non-existent?

Another question requiring attention is whether this overall decline in Part I crimes is real or whether it could be the result of some agencies deliberately reclassifying Part I crimes as Part II crimes in order to foster an appearance of success. If so, what will be the impact on community trust? How would this affect an organization's ability to document and track crime and offenders properly, to ensure victims are provided services, and to deal with offenders? And if the trend is truly what it appears to be on the surface, are police leaders appropriately adjusting and redirecting resources to respond to this shift in crime so as to remain responsive and accountable to the community? If they are not doing this, what impact does that have on police effectiveness, the budget, and community confidence?

Conversely, if we accept that the current Part I crime rate reduction is attributable, in part, to the policing strategies and crime policies that have been adopted, what might this mean for police organizations in the future? Will we leave our existing structures and

> The composition of the workforce in police agencies will also be an issue...in the coming decade.

* * *

resources as they have been, in spite of the fact that Part I crimes may have significantly declined and the workload in those areas has diminished? Or will we adapt by restructuring and redeploying our resources to respond to the shifts in crime by reassigning staff from areas where crime has been reduced to areas where it is on the rise?

The composition of the workforce in police agencies will also be an issue to address in the coming decade. For several decades, a gradual shift in police staffing has been occurring in parts of the United States (most notably in the far west region) with more agencies employing civilian personnel to provide services that were traditionally provided by sworn police officers. The primary factor influencing this has been economics, based on the desire to maintain services in the most cost-efficient manner possible. However, during the course of budget cuts in many jurisdictions, elected officials have been tending to eliminate civilian positions rather than sworn officers.

Along with the changing nature of crime, other influences are also at work that may drive more consideration of the use of civilian personnel and various non-traditional approaches. As crime increases in those areas that require unique knowledge and particular expertise, such as financial crimes and accounting skills, computer technology and systems, and other complex cases, police organizations will probably have to rethink whether the employees handling these cases are most likely going to be found within the ranks of their existing personnel or recruited from new applicant pools.

Will it be more effective and efficient to hire police officers as has been done in the past and then train them to handle assignments they may not have an interest in or be willing to make a long-term commitment to? Or might it make more sense to recruit from the ranks of accounting or IT professionals and others who are not necessarily interested in being a sworn officer but who possess valuable skills and have an interest in this work? Why not consider hiring them to supplement or complement sworn personnel who handle the enforcement functions? There is little difference to be found in this approach than with what we observed approximately 30 to 40 years ago with the hiring of the first civilian community or police service officers, crime scene technicians, forensic technicians, and a host of other assignments that are now commonly filled by capable and professional staff who are not sworn police officers.

Some of the greatest challenges for police leaders today stem not just from dealing with external factors, such as crime and service demands, but equally so from the responsibility and pressures associated with examining organizational performance in an era of increasing scrutiny. That requires a willingness on the part of police executives to ask tough questions of others in the organization and ensure the answers provided are objective and supported by facts. Are we effective? Are we accountable? Are the results that we are seeking what the community expects? Are we doing the right things? The answers will tell the story.

Ultimately, policing always has been and will be about people—the community as well as the members of the organization—and whether the latter are serving the former. ★

Joseph Brann is the founder and president of Joseph Brann & Associates, a California firm that specializes in improving organizational performance and accountability of public safety agencies. He has also served as a federal court special master and consultant to the State of California, Office of the Attorney General, monitoring and overseeing police reform efforts of local police departments. In 1994, Brann was appointed as the founding director for the Office of Community Oriented Policing Services in the U.S. Department of Justice. He was appointed by President Clinton to create and administer that agency following passage of the 1994 Crime Act legislation and served in that capacity until 1999. Brann began his law enforcement career in 1969 with the Santa Ana (California) Police Department. In 1989, he was appointed as chief of police in Hayward, California. He earned his bachelor's degree in criminal justice from California State University, Fullerton; a master's degree in public administration from the University of Southern California; and is a graduate of the FBI National Academy.

* * *

What Gets Measured Is the Matter: The Need for Leading Public Safety Indicators

by Michael S. Scott

I t is sometimes said that what gets measured matters. To turn the phrase, much is the matter with what gets measured in the crime, policing, and public safety realm.

The Federal Bureau of Investigation, in its annual Uniform Crime Reports, appropriately cautions readers not to use the data to compare police agencies; many factors outside the control of police agencies affect reported crime rates. Sound as this caution is, it is seldom heeded by journalists who write stories about police agencies, by citizens who read those news stories, by political leaders who oversee police agencies, or by police executives who administer and lead them. Like it or not, for over 80 years, the Uniform Crime Reports remain for all intents and purposes the only real game in town for rating local police departments and gauging public safety and security.

...we are foolish to persist in our belief that any single index could provide us with a reasonably accurate portrait of the quality of our police...

* * *

That the Uniform Crime Reporting Program—and even its new and improved cousin, the National Incident-Based Reporting System—provides an incomplete and sometimes inaccurate measure of crime, policing, or public safety should be beyond dispute among knowledgeable police executives and criminal justice scholars. Its deficiencies are legion: it misses unreported crime, improperly recorded crime, the noncriminal and non-law enforcement work done by police, citizens' perceptions of their safety and security, and the "apples-and-oranges" nature of different types of jurisdictions.

But acknowledging the limitations of this, or any, reported crime index is not an indictment of the index itself. The National Incident-Based Reporting System represents a substantial and important improvement over the Uniform Crime Reporting Program, which itself was a substantial and important improvement over what preceded it. The indictment to be handed down is that we are foolish to persist in our belief that any single index could provide us with a reasonably accurate portrait of the quality of our police or the safety and security of our communities.

Think of the social, economic, and physical spheres of our lives in which measuring current conditions is important, and compare how we do that with how we measure conditions in the policing and public safety sphere. When we want to know how the economy is doing, we turn not to one measure but rather to a composite index of leading economic indicators, which incorporates measures of work hours, manufacturing, unemployment, consumption, construction, stock prices, credit, interest and bond rates, and consumer expectations. When we want to know about the weather, we gauge temperature, humidity, precipitation, air pressure, wind, and cloudiness. When we want to know about the public health of communities, we measure the prevalence and transmission of disease, injuries and premature fatalities, longevity, infant mortality, exposure to toxins, access to medical care, diet, and physical activity. When we decide where to live, we assess home prices or rents; the size and design of the home; proximity to schools, churches, shops, parks, and transportation lines; demographics of neighbors; and risks to our safety, security, and peace of mind, which includes not only crime but also noise, odors, and traffic. In short, citizens can handle some complexity of measurement for important matters; indeed, they insist upon it for helping them to make important decisions.

Measuring policing and public safety is important to a variety of individual and government decisions. These measures influence where people choose to live, work, and recreate. They influence whether citizens trust the police and government. They influence how public funds are expended, both how much gets spent and on what within jurisdictions and which jurisdictions get funds. And they influence decisions about whether police funding, personnel, policy, or practice need to improve or whether other systemic changes are needed to improve public safety.

Policing and public safety measures also influence the myriad operational decisions that police officials make, including how to allocate resources and how to design strategies and tactics. At least some of the manipulation and distortion of Uniform Crime Report data by police, and some of the police tactics that diminish civil liberties and generate enormous costs to the criminal justice system, can be attributed to the pressure placed upon police administrators, and ultimately upon police officers, to drive down the Uniform Crime Report numbers. If the numbers were not given such weight by journalists, politicians, and police executives themselves, the police might feel freer to employ less aggressive strategies and tactics that are at least as effective yet more equitable.

At the broadest and perhaps most profound level, measuring crime, policing and public safety informs us about the strength and viability of our democracy: whether justice is established, domestic tranquility insured, the common defense provided, the general welfare promoted, and the blessings of liberty secured. The police subsequently came into being as a means of achieving and preserving these existential goals set out by the U.S. Constitution's authors.

The development of an index of leading public safety indicators is long past due. One should be developed that gives the same degree of careful consideration and reliable measurement to policing and public safety that has been given to other spheres of community life. Just as multiple phenomena are measured in other spheres, so too should the measure of policing and public safety comprise more than crimes recorded by police.

What else matters? In general terms, the police should be measured both by their effectiveness in achieving their objectives and by their fairness in achieving them. As it relates to effectiveness, in addition to measuring crimes recorded by police, an index of leading public safety indicators should also include measures of crimes that may have gone unreported to the police,[1] public health records of intentional and accidental injuries and deaths, insurance industry records of claims arising out of criminal conduct, noncriminal complaints about unsafe or disorderly conditions, and citizen perceptions of their personal and community's safety and security.

As it relates to police fairness, the index should measure such things as citizen trust and confidence in the police; perceptions of police fairness from lawyers, judges, prosecutors, defense counsel, civil rights attorneys, and activists; citizen complaints against the police, including civil lawsuits filed and judgments rendered; and government lawsuits filed against police agencies, such as federal pattern-and-practice lawsuits.

Each indicator—and others not mentioned—requires careful consideration as to how the data is to be collected, how it should be categorized and analyzed, how its reliability is to be demonstrated, how it is to be weighed in a composite index, and how it is to be reported. Police and crime scholars should play a role in developing the leading public safety indicators; federal, state, and local governments should play a role in collecting, analyzing, and reporting the data; and professional police organizations should play a role in vetting the system and endorsing its credibility.

Over the past 40-plus years, the American police have made tremendous strides in reconsidering and improving their relationship with the citizenry and with other government and nongovernment organizations.

They have likewise made tremendous strides in improving their understanding of the causes of crime and disorder as well as what actions, by police and others, can most effectively control and prevent them. The police have made great progress in recognizing that they alone cannot control and prevent all public safety problems, that others must share in that responsibility. And the police have made great progress in recruiting and hiring a police workforce that better reflects the communities it serves, and in training its officers how to police intelligently, compassionately, and with judgment and restraint. A remaining relic of the past, however, is the simplistic and unreliable system in place for measuring how police agencies perform. This system is undermining progress on all other fronts and begs for a long-overdue overhaul. ✸

Michael S. Scott is a clinical professor at the University of Wisconsin Law School and the director of the Center for Problem-Oriented Policing. He was formerly chief of police in Lauderhill, Florida; served in various civilian administrative positions in the Metropolitan (St. Louis, Missouri) Police Department, the Fort Pierce (Florida) Police Department, and the New York City Police Department; and was a police officer in the Madison (Wisconsin) Police Department. He was a senior researcher at the Police Executive Research Forum in Washington, D.C., and in 1996 he received PERF's Gary P. Hayes Award for innovation and leadership in policing. He holds a law degree from Harvard Law School and a bachelor's degree from the University of Wisconsin–Madison.

Endnotes

1. The National Crime Victimization Survey, provided by the Bureau of Justice Statistics, measures this at the national level, but it must be extended routinely to the local level.

Section Two

"In the year 2022, the bulky, temperamental, mobile data terminals that occupy a good portion of the front passenger compartment in a squad car will be in the police department's museum."

— J. Scott Thomson

★ ★ ★

No-Boundaries Policing

by Kriste Kibbey Etue

Mobile, flexible, and regional: three attributes successful and progressive law enforcement agencies must adopt to survive and prosper in the future. The nation's criminal justice community, and law enforcement in particular, is steeped in tradition and often resistant to change; however, with increasing demands and decreasing resources, maximizing technology and promoting both intra- and inter-department cooperation will be crucial for police departments that want to provide the highest quality law enforcement services.

In 2012, mobility is defined as an officer's ability to physically move from one location to another in a timely manner. In 2022, mobility will be a concept where the officer's jurisdiction, technology, and communication tools are all integrated to promote no-boundaries policing.

In 2022, mobility will be a concept where the officer's jurisdiction, technology, and communication tools are all integrated to promote no-boundaries policing.

* * *

In 2012, Michigan is a state with dozens of disparate and proprietary communication systems that do not easily interconnect, resulting in most Michigan State Police patrol vehicles having at least two separate radios. Without the ability to communicate across systems, the mobility of troopers to be deployed across geographic boundaries is limited. In 2022, this will no longer be an issue because all radio systems will be fully integrated and share a common platform. A patrol vehicle will need only one radio for the trooper to communicate to dispatch authorities in any of Michigan's 83 counties.

Mobility will also be fostered through in-car technology that will optimize the trooper's time on patrol. In 2012, troopers are beginning to utilize mobile applications such as electronic traffic citations and traffic crash reports. By 2022, troopers will have a one-stop-shop records management system that will incorporate all common administrative needs, including time accounting, report writing, form completion, and

data collection. Troopers will also have direct access to sophisticated biometric information that will make hiding one's identity nearly impossible.

With mobility greatly enhanced, both the trooper and agency will need to become increasingly flexible regarding assignments and responsibilities. In 2012, most troopers begin and end their day from an established Michigan State Police work site through which their activity is tracked and they complete paperwork and other administrative obligations. In 2022, most troopers will begin and end their day from home. With improved and reliable in-car technology, troopers will be able to complete most, if not all, of their reports and investigative research from their patrol vehicle, or "mobile office." The assignment of vehicles coupled with working from home will not only be more efficient but also undoubtedly increase patrol visibility and crime deterrence.

In 2012, the Michigan State Police is in the early stages of implementing the Data-Driven Approach to Crime and Traffic Safety. Deployment of resources based upon this formal approach is dependent upon reliable crime statistics being submitted in a timely manner. Currently, most Michigan crime data is submitted weeks or months after the fact. By 2022, crime statistics will be reported for intelligence analysis and resource deployment on a real-time basis, and troopers will receive their daily, or even hourly, assignment based on this timely information. True data-driven policing promotes increased flexibility for both the officer and department in deployment options and allows proactive hot spot policing, which has a significant deterrent effect.

Troopers and sergeants, the backbone of our agency, will need to become more flexible as they are weaned from the vestiges of traditional "bricks and mortar" policing. They cannot, however, be expected to do this on their own. The department must be pro-active in offering our members state-of-the-art training so they have the tools needed to succeed in this new environment. Updated training in investigative techniques, patrol tactics, leadership, and management must be offered remotely and conveniently to increase participation and decrease the costs associated with conventional classroom-based training. Embracing new training techniques will be a key to preparing our current and future troopers to succeed in 2022.

With resources becoming increasingly scarce and pressure mounting on police departments to put more officers on the streets while reducing command or desk staff, regionalization will have a significant place in 2022 policing. Since its inception in 1917, the Michigan State Police has always had a regional focus due to its statewide jurisdiction. However, the department fully embraced this concept in late 2011 with the implementation of the Regional Policing Plan. The Michigan State Police closed over half its posts, moved over 100 administrative sergeants into a mobile supervision role, implemented a squad-based trooper deployment model, and entered into dozens of cooperative, resource-sharing agreements with local police departments.

While still in its infancy, the regional policing plan is already proving beneficial to Michigan's citizens, as these efforts have increased administrative

> **Troopers and sergeants, the backbone of our agency, will need to become more flexible as they are weaned from the vestiges of traditional "bricks and mortar" policing.**

★ ★ ★

efficiencies, provided increased patrols and field supervision, and enhanced working relationships with law enforcement partners. By 2022, the Michigan State Police will have fully implemented the regional policing plan and further reduced the number of physical work locations due to enhanced technology, connectivity, and all troopers and road sergeants having assigned patrol vehicles.

Departments that maintain the flexibility to mobilize officers, either short-term or long-term, to provide police services to a region that has experienced a loss in police protection or an escalation in violent crime is a necessary and critical component of policing in the future. The Michigan State Police plans to excel in this endeavor so its services will be in demand in 2022 and beyond, as jurisdictional boundaries continue to blur, resources remain limited, and crime becomes ever increasingly mobile.

Some things will remain the same; troopers in 2022 will not look different than they do today. They will proudly wear the traditional Michigan State Police uniform, drive patrol vehicles with the red "bubble," and honor those who came before them with excellence, integrity, and courtesy. However, the trooper of 2022 will be better trained, better equipped, better managed, and fully capable of handling criminal incidents anywhere in the state of Michigan. The trooper of 2022 will begin and end the work day from home, be dispatched to an area of patrol determined not by a hunch but by real-time crime data, and have in the patrol vehicle all the tools needed to handle most criminal incidents. ★

Colonel Kriste Kibbey Etue

Colonel Kriste Kibbey Etue was appointed to the cabinet-level position of director of the Michigan State Police by Governor Rick Snyder on January 9, 2011. Etue is the 18th director in the 94-year history of the department, and she is the department's first female director. As director, Etue also serves as state director of Emergency Management and as Michigan's homeland security director. The Michigan State Police is a full-service law enforcement organization with approximately 2,400 enlisted and civilian employees. Etue began her career with the Michigan State Police in 1987, graduating as a member of the 101st Trooper Recruit School. She has served at every rank in the department. Etue holds an associate's degree from Kalamazoo Valley Community College in Michigan and is a graduate of the 206th session of the FBI National Academy in Quantico, Virginia.

★ ★ ★

Focusing on What We Can Control

by Darrel W. Stephens

On what basis can we project ourselves 10 years in the future and imagine what policing might look like? Thinking about the future often conjures up the image of gazing into a cloudy crystal ball that gradually clears and provides a picture of what might take place in ensuing years. If only that was possible… our 401(k) results would be much better.

Everyone has heard the saying that the best predictor of the future is the past. I don't recall who said this, but it makes a lot of sense. Thus, one approach is to look at recent history and use that to develop a picture of what the next 10 years might bring for policing. Certainly demographic trends can provide considerable insight into what the population will look like in the future. However, one only has to look at the advances in technological innovation and the continued expansion in how we use the Internet to understand that predicting the future based on the past has significant limitations.

53

> Developing an image of how things could look provides the opportunity to take positive steps toward creating a better future for policing.

* * *

Another approach is to describe how one would like policing to look in 2022. That crystal ball would largely be a reflection of one's aspirations for the future of policing. Such a vision would also require narrowing the broad idea of policing to some areas that seem particularly important to its future as a whole. Developing an image of how things could look provides the opportunity to take positive steps toward creating a better future for policing.

Four areas are of particular importance to the future of policing—human resources, technology, communication strategies, and collaboration. Other important areas—the economy and public policy in areas such as education and immigration—will also influence how policing will look in 2022. Although the police can influence public policy, they have less ability to control the outcomes, and their impact on the economy comes primarily from the reduction of losses associated with crime and traffic crashes and perhaps their contribution to a sense of safety.

So, the focus here will be on the four areas police have a better ability to exercise some measure of control:

Human Resources

The number of police officers in America experienced steady growth from the mid-1980s through 2008 when the economy took a downturn that has been called the Great Recession.[1] Since then, the police have experienced significant reductions in both sworn and non-sworn personnel. Studies conducted by the International Association of Chiefs of Police, Police Executive Research Forum, Major Cities Chiefs Association, National League of Cities, and others have reported furloughs, hiring freezes, and layoffs resulting in an overall reduction of police staffing.[2]

What does this mean for policing in 2022? Will the economy rebound and provide resources to allow police staffing to return to previous levels or higher? Although our crystal ball is cloudy, the costs of policing have increased so dramatically in the past (quadrupled 1982 to 2006) that staffing levels are unlikely to return to those of 2008 and may drop even lower.[3] The proportion of sworn employees in policing by 2022 is very likely to shift from a majority to a minority.

Police salaries and benefits have been a key focus for balancing budgets over the past few years. Pension benefits have been reduced for many new officers, and salary freezes have mitigated cost increases. But the only way to manage personnel expenses that represent 85 percent or more of the budget is to cut the numbers or change the mix to more lower-cost employees.

Furthermore, police officers in 2022 will focus more on work requiring sworn authority while being supported by technology and teams of non-sworn employees with special skills and training to do work that police officers do today. One can imagine geographic areas of the community being served by teams of people from police, city, and county agencies that work together to create safe neighborhoods.

Technology

Advances in technology have made important contributions to improving police effectiveness over the past couple of decades. The police are in a much better position to identify and respond to crime problems. Predicting crime events is becoming a reality and by 2022 will contribute to overall community safety. Though policing is dangerous work, improvements in equipment have contributed to reduced injury and death rates. And we have seen advances in the use of technology as a deterrent to crime, such as cameras in neighborhoods and businesses.

There is every reason to believe those advances will continue and by 2022 both police productivity and community safety will be significantly improved through the use of technology. It also offers the potential for improving officer safety through equipment and better information.

Advances in technology will also bring significant challenges and new safety threats. There has been an explosion of Internet crime and fraud that law enforcement struggles to address—by 2022 we will see increased resources devoted to this area and laws that support local police investigations and prosecution.

Communication Strategies

Changes in the news media over the past 20 years have been amazing. Newspapers have downsized as readers have shifted to the Internet and left them with a business model that no longer fits today's world. Television news competes with both the Internet and cable, providing hundreds of choices for news and information. The police have historically relied on the traditional news media to reach their communities but are now in a position where that strategy is not sufficient to keep pace.

Effective policing in 2022 will require communication strategies that are in tune with the manner in which people obtain information. How that might look in 2022 is impossible to tell—Facebook with 900 million subscribers began in 2004, and Twitter and YouTube were launched in 2006. The police will have to adjust their communication strategy continually if they expect to connect effectively with their communities. The Boston Police Department is setting the tone with the creation of BPDNews.com, which serves as the source for news on the police and crime in the community. Milwaukee and Seattle have followed suit and launched their own web-based news and information sites. All of them rely on social media as a key part of their strategy to reach their audiences.

Collaboration

Collaboration has always been a key component of community problem-oriented policing. Stakeholders partnering with the police to take the steps required to minimize opportunities to commit crime—this is an essential aspect of crime prevention efforts.

> ...police officers in 2022 will focus more on work requiring sworn authority while being supported by technology and teams of non-sworn employees with special skills...

*   *   *

As such, policing in 2022 will require collaboration on many fronts—including technology—and will be of greater importance than today. Those who do not collaborate technologically on shared goal platforms will not survive.[4] The community's sense of safety will require more than the ability to walk through the neighborhood at night—it will also require confidence that electronic financial transactions are secure and private information remains that way in the ever-expanding cyber world.

Community policing has taught the police about the importance of working with the community and other government agencies to create safe neighborhoods. In fact, the future will require a greater investment in collaboration by the police; it will require them to embrace the role of fostering collaboration between government agencies, the private sector (including security professionals), community groups, and individuals.

Conclusion

An image of policing in 2022 is difficult to construct even though it is only a decade away. To be sure, the police will have to be even less independent and more focused on collaboration to remain relevant. As crime changes, the reliance on police presence and retrospective criminal investigations will have to give way to greater emphasis on influencing the public and the private sector to take the steps that only they can take to ensure their safety. Clearly the future will bring both opportunity and challenges for policing as technology gets better and understanding the causes of crime improves. ★

Darrel W. Stephens

was appointed the executive director of the Major Cities Chiefs Association on October 1, 2010. He is also a faculty member of the Division of Public Safety Leadership in the School of Education at Johns Hopkins University, where he has served as an instructor since June 2008. Stephens is an accomplished police executive with over 40 years of experience. His career began as a police officer in Kansas City, Missouri, in 1968. He has 22 years of experience in a police executive capacity, including almost nine years as the chief of police of the 2,100-member Charlotte-Mecklenburg (North Carolina) Police Department. In addition to his police experience, Stephens served for two years as the city administrator in St. Petersburg, Florida, and as the executive director of the Police Executive Research Forum from 1986 until 1992. Stephens also served as the president, vice president, and legislative committee chair of the Major Cities Police Chiefs Association while chief of police in Charlotte. Throughout his career, he has taken on difficult and challenging opportunities and championed strategic technology investments to enhance employee productivity. He has written extensively about policing and is a frequent speaker advocating progressive policing approaches. He received the prestigious Police Executive Research Forum's Leadership Award and the Academy of Criminal Justice Sciences' O.W. Wilson Award. Stephens was elected a fellow of the National Academy of Public Administration in 2005 and is frequently called on to participate in study panels. In 2006, he was awarded an honorary doctorate of laws from the University of Central Missouri (formerly Central Missouri State University). Stephens was inducted into the Evidence-Based Policing Hall of Fame in 2010 and also received the CEBPD Distinguished Achievement Award in Evidence-Based Crime Policy.

Endnotes

1. *The Impact of the Economic Downturn on American Police Agencies* (Washington, D.C.: U.S. Department of Justice, Office of Community Oriented Policing Services, 2011), www.cops.usdoj.gov/ric/ResourceDetail.aspx?RID=619.

2. Ibid.

3. Gascon, George, and Todd Foglesong, "Making Policing More Affordable: Managing Costs and Measuring Value in Policing," New Perspectives in Policing (Washington, D.C.: U.S. Department of Justice, National Institute of Justice, 2010), www.ncjrs.gov/pdffiles1/nij/231096.pdf.

4. Bratton, William, and Zachary Tumin, *Collaborate or Perish! Reaching Across Boundaries in a Networked World* (New York: Crown Business, 2012).

★ ★ ★

Law Enforcement Communications and Information Technology of the Future

by Harlin R. McEwen

S tate-of-the-art law enforcement communications and information-sharing technologies have become increasingly critical to the law enforcement community, and these technologies and services have become essential to providing the public with the protection and security it deserves.

Our law enforcement officers and other emergency professionals must have access to modern and reliable communications capabilities, including mission-critical-communications and high-speed data and video, to communicate with each other and with federal officials across agencies and jurisdictions during emergencies.

Predicting the future is often difficult. Technology has been advancing so rapidly in the past decade that it is not easy to envision what will be possible in the future. However, it is good to sometimes brainstorm

Technologies and services
have been developed…
that will enable
law enforcement
to communicate and
share information better
than ever before.

* * *

about what may be possible with a view toward influencing the development of future technology and to make the predictions a reality.

I believe the future of law enforcement communications and information sharing will be influenced significantly by legislation passed by Congress and signed into law by President Obama on February 22, 2012 (Public Law 112–96). This law has set in motion the development of a new Nationwide Public Safety Broadband Network (NPSBN). It sets the foundation for the next generation of public safety wireless broadband communications based on technology that is already being implemented for public use by the major commercial carriers.

The expectations are that the NPSBN will bring greater reliability, security, and coverage than currently provided by commercial carriers while at the same time giving public safety access to the latest commercial technologies. Public safety will manage priority access within its own network without competing for spectrum resources on the public networks that are often crowded and unavailable during major events and emergencies. And it is expected that eventually a satellite component of the NPSBN will provide coverage when terrestrial service is disrupted or in areas where terrestrial service will never be available.

The future is exciting. The next 10 to 15 years will see the development and implementation of the NPSBN, which will bring exciting new law enforcement and public safety data services and improved interoperability.

Public safety organizations like the International Association of Chiefs of Police, National Sheriffs' Association, International Association of Fire Chiefs, National Association of State EMS Officials, and the Association of Public-Safety Communications Officials International continue to provide focus on law enforcement and public safety communications issues and promote the ongoing needs of public safety personnel.

In August 2009, the National Public Safety Telecommunications Council, a federation of 15 public safety national organizations, created the Public Safety Assessment of Future Spectrum and Technology Working Group to identify public safety communications requirements for the next 10 years. The working group followed up on a 1996 final report issued by the Public Safety Wireless Advisory Committee.[1] The updated report, titled "Public Safety Assessment of Future Spectrum and Technology" (PSAFST), has just been finalized and covers 2012 through 2022.[2] The working group has done an excellent job in conducting research and using national questionnaires to collect information from public safety personnel on the real current and future communications needs of public safety.

The PSAFST report reviews the 1996 report's recommendations, comments on whether those recommendations have been implemented, and reflects on those recommendations in today's environment. The report is broken into three key areas—operations, technology, and spectrum. It sets forth more than 20 key findings and recommendations that clearly identify the significant investments that have been made over the past 10 years to improve public safety communications and interoperability and also identifies the critical needs and challenges of the future.

In the information technology arena, the Global Justice Information Sharing Initiative (Global) is sponsored by the Bureau of Justice Assistance within the U.S. Department of Justice, Office of Justice Programs. The heart of this initiative is the Global Advisory Committee consisting of volunteer practitioners who advise the U.S. Attorney General on information technology.[3] The committee has been working diligently for many years to develop information-sharing tools and requirements for improved justice information sharing. Many of the accomplishments of Global have been or are now being implemented and serve as the foundation for the future of information sharing in the realm of justice and public safety. Services like the National Information Exchange Model were started by visionaries participating in the Global process and provide a firm foundation for financial savings to

> # The most significant challenges will be a willingness by law enforcement leaders and officers to embrace change…
>
> * * *

local, state, and federal government entities as well as improved methods of information sharing.

Specialized law enforcement and public safety applications are being developed that are similar to those currently available on smart phones and devices, such as those using Apple technology, like iPhones and iPads, and Android technology.

Next-generation 911 information (e.g., text messages, photos, and video) sent to Public Safety Answering Points by citizens using smart phone devices through commercial services will eventually be able to be forwarded to law enforcement and public safety field personnel using the NPSBN.

Law enforcement apps will access FBI Criminal Justice Information Services such as the National Crime Information Center, criminal history information, and Nlets[4] hosting services just like law enforcement already has access to Department of Motor Vehicle records, driver's license and corrections photos, and computer aided dispatch and records management systems.

In summary, the future is exciting and almost unlimited. Technologies and services have been developed, or are being developed, that will enable law enforcement to communicate and share information better than ever before.

The most significant challenges will be a willingness by law enforcement leaders and officers to embrace change, and the availability of funding. Many advanced technologies and information services are already available to those willing to implement new services, but the current economic climate is a challenge that may extend well into the future. Law enforcement leaders will need to develop strategies for funding new and improved technology in this difficult economic environment. I am convinced the investment will result in improved and more efficient services while also resulting in significant cost savings. ✳

Harlin R. McEwen serves as the chairman of the Communications and Technology Committee of the International Association of Chiefs of Police, a position he has held for more than 35 years. He was a chief of police for more than 20 years, last serving as chief in the city of Ithaca, New York. Following his retirement from Ithaca, McEwen became a deputy assistant director of the Federal Bureau of Investigation in Washington, D.C. During his tenure at the FBI, he provided executive oversight for new FBI Criminal Justice Information Services, such as the National Crime Information Center 2000 project, the Integrated Automated Fingerprint Identification System, and the Law Enforcement Online system, and he traveled extensively throughout the United States and internationally, meeting with law enforcement groups and speaking at law enforcement and criminal justice conferences. He is a life member and honorary president of the International Association of Chiefs of Police, a life member of the National Sheriff's Association, and a life member of the Association of Public-Safety Communications Officials International. McEwen has written many articles and is the recipient of many awards, including the National Public Safety Telecommunications Council's Richard DeMello Award presented at the Radio Club of America and the FBI National Executive Institute Associates' Penrith Award for executive leadership.

Endnotes

1. See *Final Report of the Public Safety Wireless Advisory Committee* (PSWAC. 1996). www.npstc.org/documents/PSWAC_AL.pdf.

2. See "Public Safety Communications Assessment 2012–2022: Technology. Operations. and Spectrum Roadmap. Final Report" (Littleton. CO: National Public Safety Telecommunications Council. 2012), www.npstc.org/download.jsp?tableId=37&column=217&id=2446&file=AFST_NPSTC_Report_06232012.pdf.

3. "Background and Mission." Global Justice Information Sharing Initiative (Global). www.it.ojp.gov/default.aspx?area=globalJustice&page=1019.

4. See "Nlets: The International Justice and Public Safety Network." National Law Enforcement Telecommunications System. www.nlets.org.

★ ★ ★

Austerity Breeds Prevention

by Rick Fuentes

The International Association of Chiefs of Police polled more than 400 law enforcement leaders from state police agencies and small and mid-sized police departments, finding that nine of 10 respondents considered staffing reductions and dwindling operational budgets as the "new reality" of policing.[1] The survey also indicated that 85 percent of those polled had already reduced their budgets, with more than half identifying their financial state as a serious issue. The Police Executive Research Forum described the new reality as a "new normal," as more than 60 percent of its city departments anticipated cuts to their 2011 budget.[2] Both tell us that budget reductions have brought about fundamental operational challenges to a significant number of this country's police departments.

Strategies to predict and prevent crime are less costly than adding staff…

* * *

Fiscal austerity, when imposed upon policing, can breed uncertainty in the ranks. Demotions, layoffs, and contract negotiations that impact salaries, pensions, and benefits drive down morale and increase the pace of retirements. It is too early to assess how the new reality and norm will threaten decades of lower crime rates, particularly across the violent index crimes most associated with the use of a weapon. There are already examples that forecast bad trends. In New Jersey, some criminal street gang members have proudly flaunted T-shirts inscribed with the date of city police layoffs, with the crimes of shootings, homicides, and carjacking on the rise in those areas.

What can a police executive do to address a department's financial straits? A police department can tighten its belt either by trimming bureaucracy or by spreading fewer cops across more dots. Big points can be scored with municipal administrators and those ministering to local treasuries if deskbound officers are replaced by lower-cost but often equally qualified civilians with commensurate knowledge, skills, and abilities. That is not to suggest that everyone should be pushed into a marked black and white.

Relocating sworn officers from behind administrative desks into investigative or outreach assignments can ensure the continuation of programs that are often victims of the first cut to beef up patrols—e.g., community policing, school resource officers, and narcotics enforcement. Eliminating these programs can cause a police department to lose its healthy grip on community relations or its ability to exert sufficient enforcement pressure upon those inclined to commit crimes. Police chiefs should remember that the broad adoption of community policing strategies brought about significant crime reductions in the 1980s and 1990s and shouldn't suffer the consequences of downsized departmental missions unless all other options are exhausted.

Secondly, 77 fusion centers have sprouted up on the landscape of American policing. There is at least one in every state and more in the most densely populated regions. They have been weaned on federal financial support and guided through specific technology processes and policies that ensure privacy interests. They are the economies of scale that help police departments of all shapes and sizes do more with less. In this challenged era that demands investing in what works and moving beyond what doesn't, fusion centers are a standout. Fusion center analysts ply their trade by making sense of data in ways that help good decision makers in policing become better informed decision makers. This is especially helpful when there are many more crime dots than cops to sit atop them.

Strategies to predict and prevent crime are less costly than adding staff to lower response times or increase investigative clearance rates. If police departments are to prevent crime, it makes sense for shift supervisors to deploy their patrols where crime is most likely to occur. Predictive policing can be a highly effective and preventive strategy when risk factors such as historical data displaying crime times, dates, and locations are stacked upon other data sets such as gang member and parolee addresses, known drug corners, and hangouts such as late-night food and liquor establishments. This needs to become a core mission in fusion centers, with sophisticated software that loads, interfaces, and maps these data sets in seconds. Predictive software has already shown high levels of probability in some states and cities. Getting it up and running in all fusion centers must be a benchmark in supporting sounder patrol deployment decisions in understaffed police departments.

As fusion centers, state police agencies, and urban police continue to build their information-sharing capacity, a significant vulnerability remains in addressing matters of national homeland and hometown security. Many of America's small- and mid-sized police departments—a national population numbering well over 15,000—continue to be disconnected from the information-sharing environment. This is not an oversight; rather, it represents how 10 years of federal homeland security funding has been disbursed to those areas of the country at most risk for crime and terrorism. Now, with the numbers of police trending downward and yet some spikes in violent crime,

…crime is not just a policing problem. It also feeds off a municipality's weakness to exert discipline upon itself.

* * *

the federal government should pursue information-sharing solutions for the small department with the same passion and urgency that has brought about the growth and prosperity of the national fusion center network and information-sharing initiatives such, as the Nationwide Suspicious Activity Reporting Initiative. Without that connectivity, the country falls way short of achieving an all-hands-on-deck national information-sharing environment that can disclose precursor terror activity and fight crime without geographical blind spots.

Much more effort needs to be directed at the prevention of crime. With noticeably less police officers on the street in many cities but undiminished public expectations, it's high time for local governments to realize that crime is not just a policing problem. It also feeds off a municipality's weakness to exert discipline upon itself. Cleaning up the blight of abandoned buildings and junked cars, lighting up dark corners, and enforcing code violations on after-hours food and liquor establishments that become hideouts and hangouts restrict opportunities for crime.

Following in the footsteps of CompStat, Baltimore, Buffalo, and more than a dozen other cities and states use management accountability and risk management programs such as CitiStat and StateStat to partner all the assets of state and local government to fight crime and create other operational efficiencies.

There have been many advances in policing in the last 50 years, most of which have given police executives an ample toolbox and brought fresh perspectives and approaches to public safety. Now, after more than 10 years of state, local, and federal financial support in the name of homeland security leading to unprecedented levels of community collaboration, technology improvements, and information-sharing initiatives, shouldn't we leverage those advances to temper the effects of federal, state, and local penny-pinching? If this is as good as it gets economically for the foreseeable future, then it's certainly worth a try. ✴

Colonel Joseph R. "Rick" Fuentes was nominated by Governor James McGreevey to become the 14th superintendent of the New Jersey State Police and was confirmed on June 2, 2003. Fuentes enlisted in the state police in January 1978, serving several postings as a general road duty trooper. He served as instructor in the training academy and then as a detective and supervisor in a variety of assignments that included the FBI/NJSP Joint Terrorism Task Force, the Intelligence Bureau, and Street Gang Unit. Prior to his nomination as superintendent, he was assigned as chief of the Intelligence Bureau, overseeing nine units within the Intelligence Section. In 1993, as a result of several narcotics investigations, he was a co-recipient of the Trooper of the Year award. Fuentes holds a doctorate's degree in criminal justice from the City University of New York. He is a member of the U.S. Attorney General's Global Advisory Committee, a member of the Homeland Security and Law Enforcement Partner's Group of the Office of the Director of National Intelligence, and an appointed member of Harvard University's Executive Session on Policing and Public Safety.

Endnotes

1. *Policing in the 21st Century: Preliminary Survey Results* (Alexandria, VA: International Association of Chiefs of Police, 2011). www.theiacp.org/LinkClick.aspx?fileticket=tbBGd4RKEGE%3d&tabid=937.

2. *Is the Economic Downturn Fundamentally Changing How We Police? Critical Issues in Policing Series* (Washington, D.C.: Police Executive Research Forum, 2010). http://policeforum.org/library/critical-issues-in-policing-series/Econdownturnaffectpolicing12.10.pdf.

Embracing the Digital Coffee Shop

by Jason O'Neal

The future of policing in America is partnerships, technology, and intelligence-led policing. In these days of increased demand and decreased funding for law enforcement, we must embrace the age-old adage of work smarter, not harder. Law enforcement is about the detection and reduction of crime, which is accomplished through understanding it.

Today, our society is more connected and mobile than ever before with ready access to the Internet and transportation. Criminals take advantage of this to engage in criminal activity across an array of jurisdictions. Whether these activities are identity theft, a series of vehicle burglaries, or serial rapes taking place across communities, criminals remain many times undetected simply because of their mobility across jurisdictional lines.

Technology…has taken the process of law enforcement information sharing to a whole new level, creating now a digital coffee shop to exchange information.

* * *

Law enforcement agencies, similar to our society, reflect a balance of different interest groups that may be representative of federal, state, county, municipal, and tribal agencies, as well as specific disciplines such as drug enforcement, highway safety, or school safety. Developing partnerships among such a diverse region is not an easy task, as it requires bringing together those who can contribute and benefit all yet often times may be competing or have other priorities.

Partnerships and collaboration among law enforcement entities and professionals lead to identification of crimes and perpetrators who may be operating across jurisdictional lines. These partnerships must be built not only among law enforcement agencies from multiple jurisdictions but also among communities and the private sector to advance their mutual interest. These partnerships provide a force multiplier and amplify the reach of the law enforcement community.

In order to have a successful partnership, communication is the key. This hinges on how well we understand others and how well they can understand us. When communication fails, the result is confusion, conflict, and frustration. We must engage people as participants, encouraging discussion and feedback.

Successful partnerships provide a more efficient use of resources and lead to initiatives such as mutual-aid and cross-deputation agreements, which allow officers to provide law enforcement services and make lawful arrests within or near a jurisdiction. Officers may react immediately to observed law violations and other emergency situations without the burden of legal jurisdiction.

Partnerships also lead to information sharing, which helps law enforcement target both criminal actors as well as similar crimes across jurisdictions. Information sharing is not a new concept to law enforcement as officers have traditionally met at the county line or even the local coffee and doughnut shop to discuss crimes and criminals. There are also a multitude of law enforcement groups and associations designed to bring officers together to share information.

Technology, however, has taken the process of law enforcement information sharing to a whole new level, creating now a digital coffee shop to exchange information. Officers now have faster access to information and communicate with more people than ever before. If information leads to knowledge and knowledge to wisdom, then the question becomes what are we doing with all this information and are we experiencing fewer problems and making better decisions because of it.

We now live in a world where we are overwhelmed with more information on a daily basis than we can possibly process. Many times, excessive information results in inaction because a method is lacking for comparing and processing that information. Being exposed to so much information, almost instantaneously, without knowing the validly of the content and with the risk of misinformation can cause disorientation and lack of responsiveness. Particularly when we view the information received as most often being irrelevant or unrelated, it becomes difficult for a person to both understand and make decisions based upon that information.

More and more law enforcement agencies are enacting policies, procedures, and training for gathering and assessing essential information. While computers may assist with analyzing these large amounts of data, it is still raw and has limited intelligence uses. For information to be useful, both the content and context must be processed. Therefore, some agencies are employing crime analysts who can digest the vast amount of information, which can be collected through various methods such as a human sources, electronic sources, or even imagery.

Intelligence can be used to understand past behaviors and forecast probable, future behaviors. Intelligence-led policing harnesses the power of this information and can be used by an officer or executive in recommending courses of action. Intelligence provides law enforcement with trends, a targeted approach to crime control, and reliable methods targeting crime prevention. It also enables the identification of persisting and developing problems.

Intelligence, if used correctly, can prove to be a powerful crime-fighting tool.

*　*　*

Advances in technology and information sharing require a responsible approach and management to ensure information is not released inappropriately. Law enforcement's goal is not only to protect the public from crime but also to ensure people's civil liberties are not violated. Privacy requires balancing the interests of the justice system with an individual's rights and public confidence.

Intelligence, if used correctly, can prove to be a powerful crime-fighting tool. And with such a powerful tool comes the responsibility to use it appropriately and ensure legal safeguards are provided to our citizens to protect privacy and civil liberties at every level.

By developing partnerships and increasing our communication and information sharing, we begin the process of intelligence-led policing, which will help ensure our justice system works stronger, faster, and smarter. This is the future of law enforcement in America. ★

Jason O'Neal is currently the deputy associate director of the U.S. Department of the Interior, Bureau of Indian Affairs, Division of Drug Enforcement. From 2004 to 2012, he served as the chief of police for the Chickasaw Nation Lighthorse Police Department, which includes a jurisdictional territory of more than 7,648 square miles in south-central Oklahoma and encompasses all or parts of 13 Oklahoma counties. O'Neal has more than 17 years of practice as a law enforcement officer, beginning as a military police canine handler in the U.S. Marine Corps; he handled both narcotic- and explosive-detector dogs. During this time, he was assigned to operations with the U.S. Secret Service on executive protection throughout California and Nevada. He also worked as a supervisory police officer in the U.S. Department of the Interior, Bureau of Indian Affairs for six years; he was responsible for the enforcement of federal, state, and tribal laws throughout a number of reservations in Colorado, New Mexico, Utah, Arizona, and Oklahoma. O'Neal is a member of the East Central University Campus Initiative to Reduce Crime Against Women, as well as multiple state councils and boards concerning violence against women, emergency management, interoperable communications, and law enforcement education and training. He is also the legislative liaison to the National Native American Law Enforcement Association and a member of the International Association of Chiefs of Police Indian Country Law Enforcement section and Firearms Committee; the U.S. Department of Justice, Senior Level Interagency Advisory Group's Tribal Working Group; FEMA's National Incident Management System Patrol and Security Working Groups; the Global Privacy and Information Quality Working Group; and the FBI Criminal Justice Information Services Division North Central Working Group, and the National Instant Criminal Background Check System subcommittee. O'Neal was named the 2008 and 2011 Chief of Police of the Year by the National Native American Law Enforcement Association.

★ ★ ★

The Role of Language in Expanding Private Sector Partnerships

by Jason Smith

Policing in 2022 will be influenced by our ability to share information through an expanded intelligence community that includes the private sector. While September 11th radically modified our capacity to share information, this process is still evolving.

Over the last two decades, we have witnessed many law enforcement strategies, including community oriented, hot spots, and broken windows policing. While each of these represents a contract between the community and the police, there is no guarantee they will endure. New strategies get published and become more attractive than the current one, and poorly managed strategies cause failure or unremarkable results. Any of these factors will diminish sustained strategic application or the eagerness for participation in a new strategy.

Information sharing is a noble banner that creates and sustains partnerships at all levels of government and the private sector.

★ ★ ★

The most innovative police departments still rely on history to manage operations and deployments; predictable human behaviors and outcomes serve as the baseline for staffing and resource allocation. Yet we have seen that this strategy can become complicated by unpredictable and reduced budgets. Police agencies change the way they do business when there is less money. Budget cuts have resulted in layoffs, furloughs, and reductions to technology, training, and initiatives designed to focus on specific crime problems.

A smarter way of using existing resources and creating a contingency for an unpredictable future is a well-executed intelligence-led policing strategy that leverages regional partnerships. The Milwaukee (Wisconsin) Police Department has institutionalized an intelligence-led policing approach that goes beyond the mere collection and analysis of information. The agency has mastered the ability to share actionable intelligence at all levels of public safety, meaning the intelligence ends up in the hands of someone prepared to use it. The agency has instructed its entire sworn and civilian staff on what this work process entails. The process has also become a standard training component for new recruits and is refreshed at each in-service.

The Southeastern Wisconsin Threat Analysis Center, an Urban Areas Security Initiative fusion center,[1] covers eight counties of the state and is co-located within the Milwaukee Police Department's main operations building. The two augment each other's ability to share information over a wide area with all parties involved. This includes the private sector, which is an integral partner in preventing crime and terrorism, as private sector security polices the majority of the critical infrastructure that is privately owned in Southeastern Wisconsin.

As such, the fusion center sought in 2011 to strengthen the information-sharing environments in the private sector by offering training on how to recognize and address suspicious activity in their own environments. This responsibility of the private sector is shared among local jurisdictions, which engage in risk management and share information and response plans addressing acts of terrorism, internal and external criminal activity, natural disasters, emergency response, critical communications, and continuity of operations.

However, what an information-sharing environment needs to grow and be sustainable is often unclear. But as established points of contact between the private organization and government agency partners educate each other on their own responsibilities, processes, and gaps, the relationships and thus information-sharing environment begin to evolve. And the relationships that arise from this dialogue are the most valuable and enduring part of a partnership.

Milwaukee accomplished two objectives in its effort to create an information-sharing environment: (1) validating police legitimacy by using shared knowledge to create crime and terrorism prevention strategies and (2) creating a lasting legacy by ensuring those strategies are sustainable.

An example of the first objective is illustrated by the relationship the Milwaukee Police Department and fusion center developed with a tribal casino. In conducting a critical infrastructure assessment, the fusion center looked beyond basic homeland security preparedness protocols and discussed crime prevention and information-sharing processes to reduce the calls for service that the casino made to the police department. While this casino is one of hundreds of private sector businesses in Southeastern Wisconsin engaged by the fusion center, this partnership created preparedness, prevention, and information-sharing templates for other tribal casinos throughout the state.

In this way, the intelligence-led policing concepts that the Milwaukee Police Department provides to other law enforcement agencies throughout the region are the same concepts that have become embedded in the tailored training given by the fusion center to the private sector. The training opportunity—which

A crisis is not the time to get to know your partners.

* * *

includes bomb technicians, tactical supervisors, and other people who need to respond in a critical incident—creates a set of shared expectations from all participants, resulting in relationships that evolve during and after the training.

The second Milwaukee objective of creating a lasting legacy was accomplished through a well-executed intelligence-led policing strategy with information-sharing emphasis. For example, when the Milwaukee Police Department and the fusion center expanded a network of information sharing with other law enforcement agencies, first responders, and private sector agencies and organizations, a series of shared expectations and new understandings were developed. The private sector understood the language used by public safety and could respond to information delivered by the police department and fusion center.

Furthermore, everyone learned that information sharing is a language understood only by the groups that work at improving it, and *if* the groups work at improving it. While a law enforcement-sensitive bulletin sent to neighboring police departments looks different from one sent to the private financial community, each partner needs to understand the message of that bulletin in the same way for a cohesive and well-planned response. Improving the collective ability to share information, to receive and accurately interpret intelligence products, should happen before it has to happen. A crisis is not the time to get to know your partners.

Information sharing is a noble banner that creates and sustains partnerships at all levels of government and the private sector. The next 10 years will see continued mainstream marketing of terrorism through Al-Qaeda publications like *Inspire*, but its real domestic applications and effects on terrorism remain unknown. Crime patterns will continue to rise and fall in different geographic areas, affecting local agencies and their communities.

The next 10 years will also show not only criminals increasingly using social media but also law enforcement, only the latter will be doing so to create awareness and prevention measures for both crime and terrorism. Standards for information sharing with the private sector will evolve to create a common lexicon enabling law enforcement to share information, threats, and courses of action. And the private sector will increasingly be engaged as a trust partner and be put at the front of these investigations or be asked to participate by recognizing and reporting the precursors to criminal or terrorist activity. By expanding information-sharing capabilities to the private sector, all partners will respond to a set of similar expectations and a shared sense of responsibility and accountability. ★

Jason Smith is a captain and the intelligence commander for the Milwaukee Police Department, which includes the Southeastern Wisconsin Threat Analysis Center, one of 77 state and major urban area fusion centers. In this role, he is responsible for providing an all-crimes and all-hazards approach to preparedness and protection of the Southeast Wisconsin Urban Areas Security Initiative Region. Smith leads a diverse team dedicated to creating an intelligence-led policing environment through prevention and enforcement initiatives. A 22-year veteran of the Milwaukee Police Department, he previously supervised criminal investigation teams in homicide, robbery, and intelligence sections of the department's Criminal Investigation Bureau.

Endnotes

1. The 77 fusion centers around the country have adopted an all-crimes, all-hazards approach to intelligence collection, information sharing, and analysis.

Producing a Positive Return on Investment

by Barbara Duncan

The future of law enforcement will undoubtedly embrace and blend the successes of past and present law enforcement practices while planning for future changes that will enhance such practices. Two of the areas where change in the profession will be most profound will be in the use of technology and in the development of police-community relations.

The benefit of proactive and data-driven patrol rather than basic reactive patrol is self-evident and time proven. Accordingly, some focus and emphasis should be placed on uniformed patrol services. There is no doubt that rapidly changing and expanding technology has in many cases provided great benefit to law enforcement and by extension the community being served.

> ...agencies that can establish communitywide trust will be in better position to expend necessary financial resources on reducing violent crime even further.

*   *   *

Unfortunately, these technologies can be quite expensive and tend to demand regular service by competent personnel, thereby draining precious resources from where they are needed most. More often than not, these resources are depleted from patrol services until the point where personnel deployment appears to favor specialization over uniformed police presence in the community.

For the future, I envision and believe a trend is developing toward technologies that will actually release personnel from desk and technology maintenance-related duties so they may return to the field where the human component is most valuable. Today's law enforcement executive must be mindful of and actively seek such relevant technologies while marshalling all available resources toward the most cost-effective expenditure of funds. Current economic times have brought austerity budgets into main-line municipal operations as a routine method of operation rather than an isolated exception. Because funding sources continue to shrink, the importance of making the proper selection of technologies has moved to the top of the consideration list.

The key to developing an economically sustainable solution to the problem of finding the appropriate technology is not always clear. As advancements in technology increase at exponential rates, the solution to the problem ultimately rests with an adroit agency leader who can either educate himself on the relevant technologies and related forecasts or surround himself with technology-savvy colleagues. Gone are the days when the competency of a chief, sheriff, or commissioner rested comfortably on the mere knowledge of traditional police applications and the selection of proper in-box solutions. Indeed, the law enforcement executive of today must be able to recognize the dilemma of the technology explosion and select technology applications that will propel the agency activity forward, toward a more efficient work product. As if this task wasn't daunting enough, the executive must also hold a vision flexible enough to accommodate the enhanced technology that 10 years into the future will hold while working within the limited funding realities of today.

It also appears that the current state of economic affairs has played a part in reshaping the way some law enforcement agencies approach crime reduction. Arguably, no police program can succeed without support from all corners of the community it serves. The fact is that our profession is inextricably intertwined with the society it serves. Ten years from now, those agencies who have successfully implemented Compstat will have secured the ground they captured in pushing crime back by reworking and redefining the approach to and nature of police-community relations. Expensive police resources are best deployed based upon data, and data is best developed through healthy community relations.

This is not to say that 10 years from now law enforcement will be relegated to deliver watered-down social programs rather than the practice of traditional law enforcement activity. To the contrary, agencies that can establish communitywide trust will be in better position to expend necessary financial resources on reducing violent crime even further.

Most agencies have experienced success stories using a combination of data-driven crime deterrence applications in conjunction with non-traditional law enforcement outreach. Citizen's police academies have been tremendously beneficial in engendering a positive interaction with the public and improving the public view of their law enforcement agency. Additionally, partnering with the business community as part of a re-entry program can steer a potential repeat offender onto a new life course. Police contact with school-age children through weekly mentoring projects is having a tremendous impact on children's attitudes and perception of the police, government, and educational processes in general. To this end, a strong relationship with local educators is critical.

> The cornerstone of success for the future of law enforcement will be the ability of the agency to be viewed as competent by all cultures within a city.

*   *   *

Although these nontraditional models have proven successful in highlighting the many attributes of law enforcement, additional work in the area of relationship building is imperative. The area deserving attention and effort during the next 10 years can be found in partnership building in those neighborhoods experiencing violent crime. The cornerstone of success for the future of law enforcement will be the ability of the agency to be viewed as competent by all cultures within a city. Relationship and partnership development between police and at-risk or even failing neighborhoods can prove challenging and must be driven by the agency executive.

When a community stands behind its police department and engages in an active partnership development with the men and women serving and protecting, crime rates tend to drop. By way of example I offer the High Point Police Department in

North Carolina. In High Point, successful crime reduction efforts featuring partnerships between police, businesses, clergy, and neighborhood residents have produced tremendous results. Building relationships based upon trust between residents and law enforcement will prove to be a critical and economically sound component in future crime reduction strategies. The relationship component between law enforcement and minority communities is in need of the most attention. I believe this premise will be especially relevant as financial constraints force law enforcement to rethink resource deployment and rework initiatives to produce a positive return on investment. ★

Barbara Duncan began her career as chief of the Salisbury (Maryland) Police Department on November 15, 2010. She came to Salisbury after having risen through the ranks over the course of nearly 22 years to become the chief of police in the city of Mount Vernon, New York. In her capacity as chief in Mount Vernon, she was responsible for the day-to-day operations of an urban municipal police force in the third most densely populated municipality in the state of New York, home to 75,000 residents within 4.2 square miles. Throughout her tenure with Mount Vernon, Duncan enjoyed assignments as a uniform and plainclothes patrol officer; a patrol squad supervisor, personnel officer, commanding officer of the Training Unit, executive officer of the Support Services Division, and commanding officer of the Special Operations Division, which included the administration of Internal Affairs and the coordination of community relations. While in Mount Vernon, Duncan successfully employed crime reduction strategies based on data-driven policing combined with active community relations. These experiences have been replicated in Salisbury, and similar successes are being noted. Prior to working in Mount Vernon, Duncan obtained her bachelor's degree in criminal justice from Mercy College, New York. In 1996, she secured her law degree from Pace University, School of Law. She graduated from the 210th Session of the FBI National Academy in 2002 and also graduated from the West Point Leadership and Command school as offered by the New Jersey Chiefs of Police Association in 2008.

★ ★ ★

Putting the "Local" Back in Local Law Enforcement

by Jim Burack

We have witnessed significant progress in policing over the past half century. We have arguably rediscovered the fundamental truth of Sir Robert Peel's assertion that the police's relationship to the public is central to crime control and a peaceful society. We have embraced scholarship and the importance of basing practice on evidence in terms of what works and what does not. Yet in spite of successful new practices—such as community policing, problem-oriented policing, crime prevention through environmental design, CompStat, Broken Windows and a related understanding of quality-of-life crimes, restorative justice, community and problem-solving courts, procedural justice, early childhood intervention, and many other instances of innovative justice thinking—we have still not experienced a breakthrough in crime reduction.

> # The intimidating nature of large, impersonal... police stations is undoubtedly a deterrent to routine police-citizen interaction and communication.

*   *   *

We have generally implemented these good, new ideas in isolation but rarely have realized the benefit that might accrue if multiple advances were layered on one another with each innovation generating additional value. Is there a policing and justice structure that would facilitate the blending and harnessing of these individual advancements simultaneously?

The key is a recommitment to true local policing, particularly in urban and even suburban America. By and large, the basis of modern policing remains the professional 911-driven rapid-response model. It's designed to put a patrol car at the caller's house within minutes. It assumes that callers prefer a house call, yet many would-be consumers of police services are reluctant to "order" a police car for various reasons, such as a sense that the problem may not be serious enough to merit a police response or the caller may not want to draw the neighborhood's attention when the squad car would pull up out front.

Many police service consumers would prefer a low-key, self-initiated visit to their familiar neighborhood police officer at the local station down the block. The intimidating nature of large, impersonal, more distantly located, fortress-like police stations is undoubtedly a deterrent to routine police–citizen interaction and communication. What is remarkable is that the policing institution collectively has not critically examined this basic assumption built into the rapid-response model and asked whether the system is discouraging customers from calling or visiting before the incident occurs and when the police might be able to intervene more effectively.

Urban policing models might look to small-town America for some cues to effective policing. Interestingly, there is policing research that suggests smaller and medium-sized police agencies can be more successful than larger ones in generating resident satisfaction. A series of studies in the 1970s by Dr. Elinor Ostrom[1] and colleagues at the University of Indiana showed that the Chicago Police Department, then perceived to be a professional urban law enforcement agency, received lower levels of citizen satisfaction scores than smaller, arguably less professional and specialized police departments in comparable neighborhoods just outside Chicago city limits. One might theorize that residents in smaller jurisdictions appreciated the personal relationship they might have enjoyed with their local officers and the heightened level of police accountability and community identity that may be more likely to occur with a small department in a smaller community.

It may be that urban American law enforcement lost its historical neighborhood roots because the professional rapid-response model does not rely primarily on community support and local relationships, even though they can certainly help. The rapid-response model is premised on the fundamental assumption that efficiency and effectiveness are derived from fewer but larger fixed patrol bases and multiple patrol cars staffed by anonymous patrol officers ready to respond at a moment's notice to the scene of the crime over a widely dispersed area. There is a powerful, and perhaps not well supported, strand in American organizational thinking that institutional consolidation is a money-saver, presumably because it eliminates redundant support services. There is clearly merit to this argument, but a more sophisticated and nuanced model can be reconciled with a decentralized patrol force operating from neighborhood-based patrol stations.

A more financially sustainable model is a hybrid; high-cost specialized law enforcement support services, facilities, equipment, infrastructure, and personnel can be shared regionally by neighboring police agencies. For example, communication centers and public safety answering points, SWAT, K-9s, drug task forces, crime labs, and specialized investigators for homicides or white-collar crime are the kinds of resources that need not be duplicated. But the patrol force and investigators who have the primary function of policing a neighborhood are truly the heart and soul of American policing. Indeed, American policing culture acknowledges the centrality of patrol as the backbone of American policing; intimate knowledge of the community and its people allows the police to support community cohesiveness and confidence and ultimately build stronger, safer communities.

We have arguably created a police and justice model more concerned with organizational comfort and efficiency, premised on organizational consolidation, than with effectiveness or sensitivity for the police consumer. What if we were to re-imagine an American justice system, designed from the ground up, for the benefit of its victims, its families, even its suspects and defendants, and ultimately the community?

We would create consolidated, approachable, neighborhood-level police stations with community problem-solving courts. The facility would include an access point to a range of government, private, and non-profit wraparound social support services, particularly for first-time, at-risk youth offenders when positive interventions early in a juvenile's criminal lifecycle might preclude later, more serious criminal activity.

This model would dissolve traditional organizational silos by utilizing a case management team that would review individual cases and create tailored responses including drug and mental health treatment. Local neighborhood-level community courts can acknowledge that low-level, quality-of-life crimes that erode community standards initially degrade neighborhoods. Local courts are more likely to take the time and effort to craft meaningful responses to local crime. Officer workspaces arranged around a conference table would promote a collaborative problem-solving approach and encourage officers to "connect the dots."

Understanding that successful neighborhoods define successful cities is critical.

*   *   *

This work environment would help reinforce innovative management and training systems that encourage community problem-solving approaches such as the Police Training Officer program.

The facility itself would leverage the power of architectural design by serving as a safety and security anchor for the neighborhood. The building would be fronted in glass so the police could provide the reassuring impression that they are observing downtown activity. The design would suggest transparency and accessibility, not a Fort Apache-like presence that suggests an "us versus them" relationship. The station would include a welcoming lobby with a children's library and toys, fireplace, and rocking chairs instantly conveying a sense of community partnership. A playground next door would encourage families to treat a police station and court as a friendly and approachable institution providing a range of services to all segments of society. Reconceptualizing the design of a police station could harness the power of architecture to reduce crime[2] and suggests one way society could deemphasize other more conventional and less effective law enforcement responses.

We should ask how our policing and justice structure can support models of new urbanism, walkable communities, livability, transit-oriented development, smart growth, the creation of a sense of place, and the whole range of thinking that now underlies the success of urban neighborhoods and the renaissance of the American city. Understanding that successful neighborhoods define successful cities is critical. The essential building block of socially and economically viable and sustainable neighborhoods is public safety, which we take for granted in many American neighborhoods. But if we are to affect the most challenged American urban neighborhoods that need jobs and economic sustainability, we must think initially about crime.

The single most significant impediment to justice innovation is the scale of our justice institutions. Urban precinct houses typically serve a collection of neighborhoods that comprise a small city—a service population of 100,000 is not uncommon. Even today, a typical budget-cutting response in times of austerity is to close police stations. This is symbolic of our lack of appreciation for the strength American policing derives from community connections and our abiding but perhaps misplaced faith in the continued effectiveness of the rapid-response model.

It is not unfair to suggest that in many American jurisdictions we have effectively removed "local" from local law enforcement, and that there is little "community" in community policing. We frequently make only a cursory commitment to neighborhoods and communities. In many places we have regionalized justice services, effectively delinking communities from police, courts, and probation and parole services. What matters is a permanent, committed police presence that is scaled to the neighborhood, reinforces community cohesion, and is sensitive to local values and culture.

The confluence of these strands of police innovation, with architecture at its core, can change officers and organizational culture. When a police officer sits with a victim, witness, or suspect by the police station lobby fireplace in a rocking chair instead of in a steel chair bolted to the floor in an antiseptic interview room, organizational perspectives, approaches, and culture can change in positive ways.

This model aligns with a range of successful and promising criminal justice and urban policy innovations we know work. It especially deserves a chance to be piloted in crime-challenged urban neighborhoods that require a police and justice presence scaled to the community and integrated with community life, standing as a beacon of safety and security and catalyzing neighborhood social and economic growth. The American urban renaissance might be expanded to a broader range of needy and deserving neighborhoods if we embrace new ways of constructing and scaling the American justice system. ★

Jim Burack is the town administrator and chief of police in Milliken, Colorado. He has also served as a U.S. Senate staffer, patrol officer with the Westminster (Colorado) Police Department, and counsel and director of operations with the Police Executive Research Forum (PERF) in Washington, D.C. A U.S. Marine Corps Reserve colonel, Burack is assigned to Marine Forces Pacific, Hawaii. Previous tours include liaison officer to FEMA and U.S. Northern Command; an active duty tour in 2004 to 2005 in Ramadi, Iraq, as the civil affairs officer leading engagement with the Iraqi judiciary in Anbar Province; evaluator with the U.S. Department of Defense inspector general for investigations and for policy and oversight at the Pentagon; civil affairs team leader during peacekeeping operations in Kosovo in 1999; and military prosecutor and special assistant U.S. Attorney in Southern California. Burack has earned a doctorate's degree from the University of Colorado, a master's degree from the Graduate School of Public Affairs at the University of Colorado, Denver, and a bachelor's degree from Dartmouth College. He is a graduate of the FBI National Academy and the Senior Management Institute for Police. He is also an adjunct faculty member in the Criminal Justice Department at the University of Northern Colorado and a member of the Colorado, California, and D.C. bars.

Endnotes

1. Ostrom was named by Time Magazine in 2012 as one of the 100 Most Influential People in the World. (See the full list at www.time.com/time/specials/packages/completelist/0.29569.2111975.00.html.)

2. Katyal. Neal. "Architecture as Crime Control," Yale Law Journal 111. no. 5 (2002).

★   ★   ★

A "Back to the Future" Paradox

by J. Scott Thomson

A "back to the future" paradox within the policing profession will come to fruition by 2022. As bleeding-edge technology rapidly becomes more affordable, simpler to use, and fitted to the palm of nearly every person's hand, the role police officers play in society, in light of the global economic downturn, will return to the 180-year-old Peel principles that are underpinned by problem solving and crime fighting.

There is not a sector of society anywhere on this planet that has not felt the impact of the current financial crisis. This change in the environment has resulted in the evolution of policing out of necessity for survival. Whether this has manifested itself in an acute form, such as layoffs, departmental closings, and regionalization, or a more chronic fashion through personnel attrition and diminished budgets, mostly all in the policing profession are feeling the constraints. The message is unequivocal; the status quo can no longer remain.

…best practices are past practices, [and] today's leaders must be vanguards of "next practices"!

* * *

The "good old days" are actually today, and police leaders must begin modifying practices and changing culture to best transition into this new normal that is currently upon many and will soon encompass all. In some regards, best practices are past practices, as today's leaders must be vanguards of "next practices"!

In early 2010, newly appointed Director Bernard Melekian of the Office of Community Oriented Policing Services for the U.S. Department of Justice forecasted four emerging components for the survival of American policing:

1. Change in the delivery of police services
2. Use of technology
3. Use of volunteers
4. Regionalization/consolidation

Melekian's soothsaying serves as a police chiefs' survival guide for the growing list of extremely challenged cities currently in the crucible, such as Detroit, Michigan, and Camden, New Jersey.

By 2022, experience will have educated society of the falsehood of the cliché "more with less" as it relates to policing. Communities will have realized that it is physically and logistically impossible to literally produce more of a service or product in an environment of increasing demands with less resources or material. Policing can and will broaden its responsibilities, raise performance standards, and demand a greater effort from its ranks. But without a fundamental change in the foundation, framework, and ideology of the police organization, the law of diminishing returns will rule the day, and success, if experienced at all, will hardly be sustainable.

This shift in the paradigm of delivering services will be accomplished well before 2022 by those who have properly managed expectations of the community and made the people themselves the catalysts of the preferred change. The transition of each other's roles in the police-community relationship will be from the most prevalent model of a customer being serviced by a vendor to a true partnership with each participant accepting greater responsibility in the process for desired outcomes.

Residents will welcome this adjustment as they enjoy the synergistic product of a concentrated police-community relationship with a narrower focus on the greatest priorities. This occurs when police agencies can no longer perform concierge-like services and cease attempting to deliver on the skewed logic of our Professional Era forefathers who guaranteed a cop to arrive at every received call. And no longer will the benchmark for success be measured solely by police response times to crimes that have already occurred.

Unrealistic demands that transform cops into clerks cannot be continued as significant reduction in resources, namely personnel, occur. The basic laws of physical science dictate that something has to give.

This transformation will not be without challenges and growing pains. However, over the next 10 years, residents will experience the value of this change in the delivery of police services by the stronger relationships they are able to develop with their neighborhood beat officer because of the officer's ability to maintain continuity of assignment. The beat cop's primary role will be protector, facilitator, and convener. When problems arise, residents will be more apt to contact their officer on his or her smart phone rather than cold call 911.

Less boots on the ground will compel police leaders to explore every force-multiplier option available to them. The private sector and military are well advanced in this area and have been using technology to enhance personnel efficiency, effectiveness, and accountability to better achieve objectives.

In the year 2022, the bulky, temperamental, mobile data terminals that occupy a good portion of the front passenger compartment in a squad car will be in the police department's museum. Officers will gaze upon it in wonderment and recall stories from their training officers about its cost and inefficiencies. The smart phones that rest on their duty belts, even in future dollars, will be a fraction of the cost and perform a greater range of tasks in a quicker, more coordinated manner that is consistent with crime fighting. They will also laugh aloud about the wasted hours of cops

hunting and pecking the QWERTY board that existed prior to the near perfection of automated speech recognition and its complete integration into the infrastructure of policing technology.

The smart phone that every officer will possess will have the ability to interact with the officer and perform an array of analytical functions, such as data mining dozens of local, state, and federal databases, centralized computer-aided dispatch records, and records management systems. Individualized biometric profiles, arrest records, wants/warrants, calls for service histories, family court, etc., will all be queried in a fraction of a second, and valuable information, offender link analysis, etc., will be articulated back to officers in a prioritized manner, giving them the ability to have a more strategic response and ultimately a more successful resolution to the matter that has summoned their attention.

These devices will automatically provide valuable, strategic street crime data or quality of life concerns based on the patrolling officer's established position via a GPS. For example, when an officer is patrolling a particular hot spot, his or her established location will trigger actionable intelligence. Succinctly receiving the spatial and temporal trends, victim/suspect profiles, modus operandi, etc., the system will give the most significant information that the street cop needs to take specific tactics to best prevent the next crime from occurring or solve a most recent event.

The ubiquitous nature of smart phones grows more each day as does the membership and usage of social media such as Twitter, Facebook, YouTube, and other networks that serve as a platform for global informing sharing. This transformation is already in full evolution, as it has reshaped how people communicate and interact with each other.

When 2022 is upon us, law enforcement will be fully engaged, from chief to rookie officer, in the use of social media and its relationship and communication with communities. To be forewarned is to be forearmed, and a circumspect public will be better positioned to target-harden themselves and provide vital information rapidly to assist in apprehending a suspect of a crime. Criminals enjoy the shadows of anonymity and will not find comfort in a networked neighborhood in a forward-leaning position against anti-social behavior.

Finally, the technological advances that enhance communication and partnership with neighborhoods will also provide a much more accurate assessment of a police officer's effectiveness. People have a right to expect 100 percent commitment from every officer honored with the responsibility of protecting the public. ✶

J. Scott Thomson has been in policing since 1992. He has been the chief of the Camden (New Jersey) Police Department since August 2008. He holds a master's degree in education from Seton Hall University and a bachelor's degree in sociology from Rutgers University. Thomson has ascended through the ranks of the Camden Police Department, serving in various operational and investigative positions and commands and receiving several commendations such as the Narcotics Detective of the Year in 1999 from the County Narcotic Commanders Association of New Jersey. He has served on the New Jersey Supreme Court Special Committee on Discovery in Criminal and Quasi-Criminal Matters and was recently appointed to the Board of Advisors for New York University School of Law's Center on the Administration of Criminal Law. In 2011, Thomson received the Gary P. Hayes Award for leadership and innovation in policing from the Police Executive Research Forum.

Car 54: Where are You?

by Bernard K. Melekian

There is little doubt that the nature of police service delivery will change profoundly over the next decade. Indeed, that change is already underway, driven in large part by the downturn in local economic conditions. A 2011 COPS Office report[1] clearly documented the loss of local law enforcement capacity as measured by the number of officer positions lost due to either layoff or attrition.

The changes to service delivery will occur across four fronts: greater reliance on technology; greater use of civilians both as employees and volunteers; consolidation among agencies, either of core services or in the form of agency mergers; and alternative delivery of non-emergency calls. Of these, perhaps the most visibly radical and most politically difficult to implement is the last, which will result in a significant alteration in the way uniformed patrol operations are conducted.

> In spite of significant personnel losses, most agencies have not changed their business model. Rather, they are doing less of the same…

*   *   *

One of the most significant changes in American policing began in the 1930s with the introduction of the radio car to uniformed patrol. Officers could respond more quickly to events, the methodology was far more economical than foot patrol, and, as post-WWII America sprawled into the suburbs, the visibility of the local law enforcement agency was maintained. Conversely, the detachment of local law enforcement from the communities they served has been directly tied to this change.

Two key tactical assumptions underlie the use of mobile uniformed patrol. The first is that the random nature of such patrol is a deterrent to crime. The second is that such patrols should cover every portion of the jurisdiction during the course of a patrol shift. While the first assumption has been substantially discredited by numerous studies over the last 40 years, such studies have not altered the second assumption for reasons that are as much political as operational.

The model has not changed since the introduction of the radio car. A person calls dispatch, the call is evaluated, a radio car is assigned, and officers handle the call. For the average citizen, the patrol response is the police department. Law enforcement has trained the public to expect a response to almost any request for service. This effort is usually seen as being distinct from community policing.

Since the introduction of community policing in the 1980s, few departments have fully implemented the concept as the foundational philosophy of their organizations. Rather, community policing has coexisted alongside the traditional reactive model for patrol. For the most part, jurisdictions were not really forced to make choices between the two operating modalities.

The changes wrought by the economy have brought this inherent tension to the surface. As agencies downsize, chiefs often say they can no longer afford their community policing programs, which indicates that community policing was a program rather than a philosophy. In spite of significant personnel losses, most agencies have not changed their business model. Rather, they are doing less of the same; that is they still use the same basic patrol response but with longer response times.

The delivery of patrol services will need to change fundamentally. This change will be driven by the loss of capacity (i.e., the number of officers available) and recognition of the fact that patrol visibility does not need to touch 100 percent of a jurisdiction's streets and neighborhoods. The work that has been done by researchers such as David Weisburd,

Andrew Papachristos, and others suggests that a more surgical approach to the deployment of patrol resources can have a significant impact on reducing the levels of crime and social disorder.

Patrol response falls into three broad categories: emergency response, order maintenance, and non-emergency responses. The time available to the patrol officer on any given day is finite. Emergency response will always be the priority for local law enforcement, but it consumes a small portion of the allotted patrol time. The remainder is divided between the other two categories.

Order maintenance activities are those duties that are seen as the desirable, proactive aspects of community policing. They include crime control, traffic management, and community outreach. The ability of the patrol officer to engage in these meaningful activities is a direct function of the amount of time available to that officer, and the percentage of non-emergency responses determines the time available.

Non-emergency responses take up the bulk of the officer's directed time. Activities such as report taking, alarm responses, and non-critical investigations fall into this category. For a variety of reasons, many jurisdictions are reluctant to seriously consider alternative responses to these kinds of calls. In this area, true changes in the delivery of patrol services will need to occur.

> …the infusion of the millennial generation into police work is creating a workforce that wants to be engaged in a more direct and creative fashion.

* * *

Patrol services will be much more place and person focused. Research—beginning with Marvin Wolfgang's famous Philadelphia cohort study and continuing through David Weisburd and Lawrence Sherman's landmark work on hot spots in Minneapolis—has demonstrated the significant impact a small number of persons and places can have on a jurisdiction's overall crime rate. The implications for the delivery of patrol services are also significant. If the research proves to be applicable to a broad range of jurisdictions, the ability to control crime and perform social order maintenance would no longer be dependent solely on an ever-increasing number of officers. Rather a much smaller group of officers could focus on these places and persons in a much more effective and cost-efficient fashion.

Three factors are converging to make true change in the delivery of patrol services a reality. First, the constriction of the economy is reducing the number of sworn officers available to handle patrol duties. Currently many departments are responding by eliminating special details such as narcotics and traffic units. The officers that were in these units are being assigned back to patrol. However, those special details actually serve a critical function that will ultimately need to be filled.

Second, the infusion of the millennial generation into police work is creating a workforce that wants to be engaged in a more direct and creative fashion. This generation demands that its work be fulfilling and that it be provided much greater latitude in setting the parameters of that work. Patrol work that requires significant research and emphasizes creative problem solving will be perfectly tailored for this new generation of officers.

Third, there is a growing recognition among law enforcement leaders that patrol is ultimately where the connection between the department and the community it serves will be forged. The actions of the patrol officers, more than any other aspect of the department, will determine the legitimacy of the department. For too long, patrol was the place where an officer began his career and worked toward leaving for a special detail. Being sent back to patrol was always considered a punishment. This is going to change.

In the future, patrol will look quite different. The non-emergency responses will be handled by civilians or by greater reliance on technology. There will be fewer patrol officers, but they will be highly focused problem solvers who will rely heavily on research to determine the focus of their daily activities. Such research will identify not only criminals but also key persons or places in the community in order to enhance the legitimacy of the agency. Their training will focus heavily on interpersonal communications and scenario-based problem solving. Their equipment will be rich on data access, and their weaponry will be heavily less than lethal. The use of force will be discreet, surgical, and effective.

The essence of police service will never change. We will always strive to protect the innocent and pursue the guilty. We will always recognize that law enforcement determines the truth or falsity of the constitution and our system of laws. In short, what we do will not change, but how we do it is going to change quite radically. I think it's going to be quite exciting. ★

Bernard K. Melekian was announced as the director of the Office of Community Oriented Policing Services by Attorney General Eric Holder on October 5, 2009. Prior to joining the COPS Office, Melekian was the chief of police for the city of Pasadena, California, for more than 13 years. He also served with the Santa Monica (California) Police Department for 23 years, where he was awarded the Medal of Valor in 1978 and the Medal of Courage in 1980. Melekian has been the recipient of numerous awards and is recognized as a leader whose commitment to the advancement of community policing is built on years of patrol experience and a strong record of incorporating the needs of the community into police operations. In April 2010, he was awarded the prestigious National Public Service Award by the American Society for Public Administration and the National Academy of Public Administration. Melekian holds a bachelor's degree in American history and a master's degree in public administration, both from California State University, Northridge. He earned his doctorate in policy, planning, and development from the University of Southern California and is also a graduate of the FBI National Academy and the California Command College. Melekian served in the U.S. Army from 1967 to 1970. As a member of the U.S. Coast Guard Reserve, he was called to active duty in 1991 during Operation Desert Storm and served in Saudi Arabia. Melekian served a second tour of active duty in 2003, and he retired from the U.S. Coast Guard Reserves in 2009 after 28 years of service.

Section Three

"We need to get this right. Forget 'Too Big to Fail.'

Our motto as we build to the future ought to be that

law enforcement is 'Too Important to Fail.'"

— Christopher Tracy

★ ★ ★

Balancing the Art and Science of Policing

by Tim J. Dolan

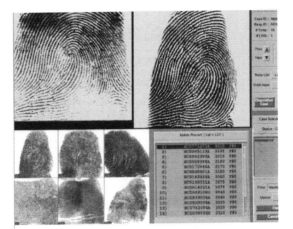

I believe a chief of police of a major city in America needs to be optimistic but always a little concerned. Being concerned or apprehensive is a survival trait learned long ago when we worked the street. Getting too comfortable could make you a little less attentive and result in a mistake that is either unsafe or, at the very least, problematic. One of the areas of policing that makes me a little nervous is the rapid development of technology. I think technology presents some of our largest future opportunities as well as challenges.

Analytical intelligence (e.g., crime statistics, mapping, and systematic observations) has led us to results-oriented policing—putting as former New York and Los Angeles Chief of Police Bill Bratton commonly called "cops on the dots." Today's advances in analysis are changing our reactive tactics to become more future-oriented and proactive. Predictive policing matches criminal intelligence with crime statistics and

Technology advances are clearly opportunities for us to police better.

★   ★   ★

intangible factors to tell us where the risk is higher for the next crime to occur.[1] For crime analysis to be fully and effectively integrated, leadership must be its champion by demanding value, having it contribute to the mission, having the right people on board, and prioritizing the technology and data quality.[2] According to Rutgers criminologist George Kelling, recent police innovations in evidence-based tactics have led the way for accountability for all of municipal government.[3] These advances, coupled with additional technologies such as ShotSpotter[4] and business and community cameras, have made us much more effective and efficient. We have, in many cases, been able to do better with less. The results show that smart policing tactics matter.

In addition to the technological advances to overall policing strategies, we have the advances available to our *employees* on the street. I use the term employee because many of today's new police department employees are specialists due to the skills needed to manage new technological advances. We have forensic scientists, crime analysts, neighborhood outreach personnel, crime prevention specialists, and more. In order to take full advantage of those advancing technologies, we will need to increase the number of these specialists.

The primary role of specialists is to make our departments and officers more efficient and effective. They let our officers know where they should be when, and they put tools in officers' hands that help them better deal with whatever they come across. It is ironic that while the need for specialists grows so does the need for our officers to become more generalists.

We all know that police officers are very expensive. Their continued support and funding depends on the quality of their community policing or their ability to serve. They need to be a "jack of all trades" when responding to calls for service. They are crime prevention experts, traffic controllers, medics, first-response tacticians, mediators, investigators, legal experts, and much more. They need the right tools to help them get dispatched, seek information, record statements, photograph evidence, collect DNA, make a report, and give advice.

In many ways, our future police officers are truly going to be Texas Rangers. The rangers' motto of "one riot, one ranger" will actually become true for most law enforcement calls for service.[5] Tomorrow's police will have more information and capacity due to computers in their squads and on their person.

Computers are already becoming the "other officer in the squad." They can track every movement of squads and officers using GPSs. Dispatchers use GPS and computer monitoring to maximize efficiencies and generate alerts. Officers can access criminal and informational data in their squads and on handheld devices.

Tomorrow's police officers will be partnering even more with computers. Computers will eventually become "partners" to any officer working the street and will work with officers in real time. Officers will get a suggested route to any call based on the latest traffic data. Traffic lights will be changed to assist with their safe and quick arrival. Business and neighborhood cameras, as well as ShotSpotter technology, will help to monitor the flight of suspects. Officers will quickly receive recorded information and get intelligence on the address and its occupants.

Once officers arrive at a scene, computers will record their activities as well as listen and watch for threats. The officer's phone camera will be able to scan and record crime scenes instantly. Phone apps will assist with collecting evidence and recording statements.

It all sounds very futuristic or sci-fi, but the truth is that most of the tools mentioned already exist and are being used to some capacity by the military and law enforcement. Connecting what we call artificial intelligence[6] into our day-to-day work will keep increasing as we find ways to integrate databases and find safe and efficient ways to store data. We only have to look at what the average person can already do with Siri on their iPhone today to get a glimpse of what connecting all our law enforcement databases and apps would mean to an officer.

Technology advances are clearly opportunities for us to police better. They help us tremendously in the science of policing. They will never, however, replace the need for police officers or what we call the art of policing. The art of policing[7] is the human side.

Training is teaching someone how to use a tool. Education is what helps an officer use a tool wisely.

*   *   *

It is what can make one officer superior to another despite the fact that they might have the same tools, education, and training.

Within law enforcement, we see the art of policing every day. It is the street officer who "just knows" this particular traffic stop is dangerous; the officer who uses discretion for the greater good; the homicide investigator who gets a reluctant witness or suspect to talk; or a chief that makes a legally non-advisable comment on an incident to quell public outcry. The art of policing comes from innate skills, smarts, experience, or traits that are inside a person. It relates to a person's ability to interact, perceive, innovate, and act.

I am concerned that the art of policing will not improve as rapidly as the science of policing—only because those technological innovations are coming so rapidly. We know that better tools used inappropriately or wrongly can be dangerous. Electronic control weapons[8] are a good example. Used appropriately, these devices can help us arrest combatants more quickly and safely. Do they take the place of lower level use of force? No. Do they eliminate officers having to put hands on resistant arrestees? No. Should they be used on any physically resistant arrestee? No. Are there crystal clear guidelines of when we should or should not use force? No. We need officers to use their best discretion of when and when not to use certain types of force.

As an administrative example, we can talk about access to state database driver's license information. Having access to this information allows officers to see the driver's photo, address, and driving record. They should not be accessing this information for personal purposes. Doing so is a violation of the driver's rights.

So, how do we ensure we are improving the art of policing with the advances of technology? I believe that education plays a major role. By education, I do not necessarily mean training. Training is teaching someone how to use a tool. Education is what helps an officer use a tool wisely. We need to make sure that our officers are well-educated and are people of strong ethical character.

Police chiefs know that any given day can bring their next major challenge. Along with good leadership, progressive tactics, advanced police education, and recruitment they will look for assistance from technology. Technology used wisely can make us more effective and more efficient. However, those fast-moving advances in technology can also present some of the greatest challenges. ★

Tim J. Dolan has served as chief of the Minneapolis (MN) Police Department since April 2006. He holds a master's degree in public administration from the University of St. Thomas and is also a graduate of the FBI National Academy and Police Executive Research Forum's Senior Management Institute for Policing. In his 34 years in law enforcement, he has also served as assistant chief, deputy chief, and commander of the Fourth Precinct, as well as commander of SWAT, Narcotics, Training and Precinct Patrol. During his tenure as chief, the department has seen historic declines in violent and Part I crimes. The department has also won international recognition and awards for their efforts in juvenile justice, community policing partnerships, downtown business partnerships, and other crime reduction initiatives. The department takes great pride in their recent successes with the 2006 I-35W bridge collapse, the 2008 Republican National Convention, and the 2011 Northside Tornado. Dolan is a life-long resident and employee of the city of Minneapolis. He has been married to Lori for 32 years, and they have four sons—Ben, Matt, Brent, and Tom.

Endnotes

1. See Egge, Jeff, "Experimenting with Future-Oriented Analysis at Crime Hot Spots in Minneapolis," *Geography and Public Safety* 2, no. 4 (March 2011), 6, www.cops.usdoj.gov/RIC/ResourceDetail.aspx?RID=598.

2. Taylor, Bruce, Rachel Boba, and Jeff Egge, "The Integration of Crime Analysis into Patrol Work: A Guidebook" (Washington, D.C.: U.S. Department of Justice, Office of Community Oriented Policing Services, 2011), 15–16, www.cops.usdoj.gov/ric/ResourceDetail.aspx?RID=617.

3. "The View from Academia: Police Chiefs Must Take a Long-Term View in Responding to the Economic Crisis," in *Is the Economic Downturn Fundamentally Changing How We Police?* Critical Issues in Policing Series (Washington, D.C.: Police Executive Research Forum, 2010), 23–24.

4. The Minneapolis Police Department has been using ShotSpotter for about nine years and has coordinated syncing ShotSpotter with its neighborhood cameras. (See www.shotspotter.com.)

5. "One of the most enduring phrases associated with the Texas Rangers today is 'one riot, one ranger.' It is somewhat apocryphal in that there was never actually a riot; rather, the phrase was coined by Ranger Captain William 'Bill' McDonald, who was sent to Dallas in 1896 to prevent the illegal heavyweight prize fight between Pete Maher and Bob Fitzsimmons that had been organized by Dan Stuart and patronized by the eccentric 'Hanging Judge' Roy Bean. According to the story, McDonald's train was met by the mayor, who asked the single ranger where the other lawmen were. McDonald is said to have replied: 'Hell! Ain't I enough? There's only one prize-fight!'" ("Texas Ranger Division," Wikipedia, last modified June 13, 2012, www.texasranger.org/history/BriefHistory1.htm.)

6. See Beukes, Johann, "Is Artificial Intelligence Truly Possible?" last modified October 25, 2011, http://johannbeukes.com/is-artificial-intelligence-truly-possible/2011/10/25/.

7. Finding a clear definition of "the art of policing" is difficult. However, renowned criminologist George L. Kelling said that "police work is complex, that police use enormous discretion, [and] that discretion is at the core of police functioning" ("Broken Windows" and Police Discretion, Washington, D.C.: National Institute of Justice, 1999, 6).

8. See Police Executive Research Forum, *2011 Electronic Control Weapon Guidelines* (Washington, D.C.: U.S. Department of Justice, Office of Community Oriented Policing Services, 2011), http://cops.usdoj.gov/Publications/e021111339-PERF-ECWGb.pdf.

★   ★   ★

Pursuing Excellence in Policing: The Leadership Challenge of the Future

by Charles H. Ramsey

The increasingly complex social, technological, and political environment in which we find ourselves places difficult demands on police organizations. More often than not, we struggle to keep pace with our ever-changing landscape. As we continue to move forward in the 21st century, what will be the next step in our evolution as a profession? How will we meet the challenges and opportunities confronting police agencies globally?

There are many contemporary issues in policing that demand our immediate and future attention if we are to stay relevant and capable in our crime-prevention and fighting mission. The more technically proficient we become at preventing, reducing, and solving crime, the more likely we will have to do so with shrinking resources. All police organizations have been affected by the economic downturn, but expectations that we continue to be just as effective in our crime-fighting

> # We need police leaders who can mobilize and inspire… not become immobilized by the uncertainty of the future.

★ ★ ★

mission remain the same, if not higher. We must rise, not only to meet the exigent demands of our globally connected society but also to set our own expectations about what is possible.

What is possible for our profession is ultimately dependent on the men and women who will become the leaders of our police departments in the future. If we don't create our own future, others will. We cannot lose sight of the fact that without talented, bold, and innovative people willing to put themselves in the highest positions in our agencies, our profession will languish and be trapped on the sidelines of our own evolution.

Developing leadership competencies in the private sector and military is a highly valued enterprise. Our nation's best business schools and military academies all have robust programs, including executive education, on the subject of leadership. Leadership is an area in which many of our corporate, government, and educational institutions invest significant resources. Our profession must do the same. Though there are programs that focus on management and leadership for police at various ranks, I believe we must develop leadership training and education programs specifically for top-level law enforcement executives.

At the center of effective leadership are competencies that are not typically found in any one discipline or taught by a subject matter expert. It is incumbent upon this generation of leaders, however, to articulate and impart these core leadership competencies to the next generation. Leaders must possess self-awareness, maintain a broad and interdisciplinary perspective, be comfortable as the focal point of a complex system, balance constant public scrutiny, develop a successful senior team, manage relentless stress, and cultivate a command presence. We must partner with premier leaders in business, government, the military, and the non-profit sector and work with our colleagues from around the world in delivering a leadership program that tackles these issues. We also need to tap into the body of knowledge from current leaders in policing and other industries to bring their experiences to life through candid and contemporary case studies.

More often than not in our profession, we cultivate leadership by accident, or good fortune, not by design. We have the opportunity, and I believe the responsibility, to help ensure the success of the next generation of men and women who will carry this profession into the future. We need leaders who will possess the technical, psychological, and emotional strengths to bring the right people together, at the right time, doing the right things for the greater good. The end result when all the individual pieces are moving in synchrony can be powerful. This is a complex process, made even more complex because of the world in which we live.

Let's imagine for one moment how an orchestra sounds at the beginning of rehearsal, where all the individual musical instruments can sound quite unharmonious, with each player moving at his or her own pace. Then the conductor assumes his position and with a series of hand gestures unifies the performers, sets the tempo, listens critically and carefully to the sound of the ensemble, communicates the vision forward, and guides them to their harmonious conclusion. We need police leaders who can mobilize and inspire their organizations to lean forward into this complex environment but not become immobilized by the uncertainty of the future.

Leading in this complex and high-risk world requires more than just an understanding of complexity; it requires a strong sense of how to thrive within it. Police leaders must be ready to fight crime and terrorism, deploy resources effectively, meet citizen needs, satisfy political administrations, and maintain organizational credibility and morale—all while under the scrutiny of a globalized media network. We cannot rely on the status quo or on chance to produce the leaders of the future. Let us take the first bold and visionary step now to create the future we want for our profession and ourselves. ★

Charles H. Ramsey, the Philadelphia (Pennsylvania) police commissioner, leads the fourth largest police department in the nation with more than 6,500 sworn members and 830 civilian members. He brings over 40 years of knowledge, experience, and service in advancing the law enforcement profession in three different major city police departments, beginning with Chicago, then Washington, D.C., and now Philadelphia. Ramsey has been at the forefront of developing innovative policing strategies and leading organizational change for the past 19 years. He is an internationally recognized practitioner and educator in his field, and he currently serves as president of both the Police Executive Research Forum and Major Cities Chiefs Association—the only law enforcement professional to hold both of these prominent positions at the same time. Ramsey holds both a bachelor's and master's degree in criminal justice from Lewis University in Romeoville, Illinois. He has lectured nationally on community policing and homeland security and received numerous awards, including the John M. Penrith Award for leadership from the FBI National Executive Institute, the Leadership in Policing Award from the Police Executive Research Forum, and the Innovations in American Government Award from the Harvard Kennedy School, John F. Kennedy School of Government.

★ ★ ★

Social Unrest, Drug Abuse, Cyber Crimes, and No Money

by David E. Dial

In the best of times, the enforcement of laws has always presented challenges for all societies. Those challenges are exacerbated during periods of rapid change. As we entered the new century in 2000, America began such a period. It is unlikely that the pace of societal changes will be slower during the next decade. To meet the challenges that are looming in the future, police leaders will need to prepare their departments for change.

The 1990s were relatively good years for law enforcement in America. Economically, the country was prosperous, technological advances enabled the use of DNA and automated fingerprint identification systems to enhance our crime-solving capabilities, and the community oriented policing practices and partnerships that started in the prior decade began to pay off with decreases in crime rates throughout most communities. Those good years did not continue.

One challenge of the future then will be continuing resource limitations.

★   ★   ★

The terrorist attacks of September 11 drove our country into a prolonged war and we spiraled into the biggest economic decline since the Great Depression.

The economic downturn of the last few years was certainly unprecedented, and it began a revolution of fundamental change in many police agencies across America. However, this financial collapse and the mandated changes were not without warning. As early as 1973, Adam Smith wrote in his bestselling book, *Supermoney,*

> *We are all at a wonderful ball where the champagne sparkles in every glass and soft laughter falls upon the summer air. We know, by the rules, that at some moment the Black Horsemen will come shattering through the great terrace doors, wreaking vengeance and scattering the survivors. Those who leave early are saved, but the ball is so splendid no one wants to leave while there is still time. So, everyone keeps asking "What time is it?" but none of the clocks have any hands.*

Anyone in this profession during the last four years knows that the horsemen have arrived. Virtually every police agency in the country has been or will be impacted by decreasing revenues. I have listened to scores of police chiefs across the country discuss the service modifications and the structural changes that have been necessitated by the new fiscal reality, and no one thinks they will have the ability to put more police officers on the street and return to the personnel resource level of five years ago. One challenge of the future then will be continuing resource limitations. Police leaders owe it to their communities to adjust to these limitations in a positive way and to provide the highest level of police service possible with the resources they have available. They will need to develop online reporting capabilities, merge resources with neighboring agencies, and use technology in ways they have not thought of in the past.

The development and use of technology to enhance our productivity is not something that we can depend on others to do. Most departments today lack the necessary software and data analysis capabilities to collect, collate, and disseminate useful information to patrol officers. Even fewer have meaningful social media strategies and capabilities for the gathering of intelligence and situational awareness. Limited resources impede their abilities to do any real strategic planning and to improve technological capabilities.

Police executives will need to look within their agencies for someone to champion these causes. Police and fire departments throughout the country have scores of employees who have tremendous technical knowledge, and they are being underutilized by the agencies that employ them. During the last decade, a Fremont, California, police officer became one of the first to develop an online reporting system, and a Naperville,

Illinois, firefighter worked with vendors to develop a regional state-of-the-art interoperable communications network. The challenge is to find out who these underutilized employees are, train them, and improve crime prevention and crime-fighting capabilities. Simply stated, get the right people on the bus, and get them in the right seats.

Closely related to the need for new skills and technology is the need for a computer forensics lab to investigate the growing number of cyber crimes. Computers, cell phones, and electronic tablets are now being used in virtually all types of crimes. Some criminals even use these devices to record their crimes. Being able to examine them forensically will be a critical part of policing in the future. To afford the necessary technology and training associated with a computer forensics lab, police agencies should consider grants, partnerships with community agencies, seizure funds, and regionalization. The upward trend in cyber crimes and the use of technology is only going to increase in the future.

Modern America is made up of a divisive citizenry. This division is greater than any time since the 1960s and perhaps more than any time since the Civil War. This divide is brought on by several issues that include the growing frustration with the Global War on Terror; differing ideas on how to handle immigration and illegal immigrants; conflicting opinions on the redistribution of wealth, health care, gun control, and the legalization of drugs; and ever-changing demographics. Increasingly, it is exhibited in anger and hostility directed at government. Although it is uncertain how our divided attitudes will impact our communities, the social conditions are ripe for widespread protests

and riotous behavior in the future. The police will be placed squarely in the middle of conflicts that will arise in the next few years. The wise police leader will have his or her organization trained and equipped to deal with sudden disorder that can erupt.

With the social networking sites that exist today, the tactics employed by protest groups and radicals will be vastly different than the ones that have existed in the past. Police agencies will be required to monitor these sites and develop intelligence networks within their communities and other agencies. They will also need to ensure that their mutual aid pacts are current and have plans in place to deploy the necessary resources rapidly and effectively to prevent widespread violence and property damage.

During the recent NATO summit held in Chicago, the police and federal law enforcement agencies wrote the book on how to handle large-scale protests in that city. They monitored websites and gathered intelligence about what to expect, ensured the protection of protestors' constitutional rights, and made clear boundaries about where the protests could occur. The officers were equipped, trained, and ready to handle any disturbance that might arise. No one should think, "It can't happen here."

In many parts of the country, illicit drug use is on the rise again. This is not a good trend, and it is something that police agencies should do everything they can to get this problem under control. Families are being destroyed, and many people, mostly young, are dying from drug overdoses. I served as the chief of police for 22 years in the nice Chicago suburb,

Naperville. During my final year of service as chief, we recognized a significant increase in the abuse of heroin by teenagers. In 2011, eight people died of heroin overdoses in our community. Four of them were students at one specific high school.

We quickly recognized that this was not a problem the police department alone could solve. In addition to increased undercover enforcement, two of our detectives formed partnerships with the local hospital, both school districts serving our community, social service providers, and homeowner groups. A powerful, factual community presentation about the impact of drug abuse and addiction received widespread publicity and was given several times at multiple locations in the city. More than 1,000 parents and teenage children watched these presentations in person and several thousand more watched the local television network showing of them.

We focused our efforts on making parents aware of how the heroin was getting into our community, what they should look for, and where they could find help. We tried to educate young people about the very real dangers associated with drug abuse. These presentations were given high praise from parents, social workers, school officials, and health care professionals. More important, we are now nearly seven full months into 2012, and we have experienced only two more drug overdose deaths this year. Our goal, of course, was zero.

Police agencies in America can expect several challenges in the next decade, but we must keep in mind that we have been challenged before. We have met those challenges with honor, dedication, and professionalism. We make a difference in our communities, and they need us to continue. ★

David E. Dial retired from service as the chief of police in Naperville, Illinois, on May 18, 2012. He served as a police officer for more than 45 years, including 22 years as chief. Dial has a bachelor's degree in law enforcement and administration from San Jose State University, a master's in public administration from the University of Colorado, and a second master's degree in homeland security and defense from the Naval Postgraduate School. He has also attended the FBI National Academy and is a graduate of the Senior Management Institute for Police sponsored by the Police Executive Research Forum. He has served on various committees throughout his career and is currently the immediate past president of Police Futurists International. Beginning in August 2012, Dial assumed the role of criminal justice director at Aurora University in Illinois.

★ ★ ★

Rethinking "Business as Usual"

by Joseph A. Schafer

American higher education has been undergoing a fundamental transformation since the mid-1990s. For-profit degree programs have grown exponentially, enabled by the rise of computer-based learning systems. More recently, we have begun to see entire college courses, often taught by leading experts in a given field, being made freely available to members of the general public. Anyone can take a course on artificial intelligence taught by a world-renowned scholar from Stanford University. Receiving transcripted college credits for that experience is not freely open, but anyone can access the lectures, study materials, and assessments used in this course.

"Business as usual" in American higher education is rapidly changing in directions we cannot conclusively predict. What these evolutions will mean for brick-and-mortar universities is unclear. What they might mean for state university systems, which have

> For years, a bright divide has existed between the corporate world…and the public sector…. Simply stated, these bedrock assumptions are no longer true.

*   *   *

endured years of declining public financial support, is unclear. Could we reach a point where young adults have completed many of the same education experiences (or possibly even better learning experiences) than those of earlier generations, but do not have a college transcript, degree, or debt load?

The trends and trajectories we can observe in higher education are helpful when considering the future of American policing, which is also undergoing a radical transformation. But the profession is not as far down this path relative to higher education. Colleges and universities are deep into an uncertain journey with an unclear future. Policing is in the early years of a similar process. In both cases, I would argue the professions need to boldly, courageously, and critically rethink business as usual. While the future may be unclear, what is evident in both professions is that old ways of thinking and operating will be decidedly inadequate for the future reality.

In May 2012, several British policing services began to explore privatizing aspects of their operations. This step was not only to privatize low-level aspects of policing in these regions but also to out-source core tasks, including routine patrol, investigations, and detention. With a starting contract price tag of over $2.4 billion spread over seven years, the announcement generated considerable interest from a number of major corporations involved in military, industrial, and public safety contracts.

Whether privatization of such services truly creates financial gains, results in better service delivery, or is in the interests of communities or citizens is irrelevant. This event signifies the death-knell of what historically has been a bedrock assumption of the public sector—that government agencies are too big to fail and too entrenched to be supplanted or replaced. For years, a bright divide has existed between the corporate world (with its emphasis on cost and value) and the public sector (populated by organizations that "had" to exist). Simply stated, these bedrock assumptions are no longer true. Legislative and executive branches, facing daunting financial realities, will increasingly look for ways to provide services at a lower cost. Whether that is prudent in the long term will be a trailing consideration to the short-term fiscal gains. Previously sacrosanct government agencies could find themselves dramatically restructured or disbanded altogether.

What this means for the future of policing is that "business as usual" assumptions about police organizations, operations, leadership, tradition, and culture must change. Calls for change in American policing can be traced back to the roots of the International Association of Chiefs of Police, the 1931 Wickersham Report, and various other inquiries arising during the past century. What has changed is that agencies that do not change by 2022 will face the real threat of elimination, something previously unknown.

To respond to these changes, American policing must initiate real, honest, and critical dialogue and innovation. Paramilitary bureaucratic organizational structures and operational approaches were vital in removing systemic corruption from policing more than a century ago. They are decidedly ill suited for modern public safety needs. Bureaucracy is slow and entrenched and resists change. It suppresses creativity, innovation, and flexible ways to address problems. In a world where technology changes at an exponential pace and society is undergoing continuous rapid transformation, agencies employing bureaucratic government structures risk being rendered incapable of addressing their core missions.

The prevailing bureaucratic command-and-control structure noted in the majority of American police agencies is the wrong model if agencies hope to attract and retain the services of those entering the modern labor market. Policing has been experiencing a recruitment and retention crisis since the mid-1990s. Efforts to correct this problem have largely failed. Today's youth are different than their predecessors, including those currently leading police organizations. Lamenting that fact has neither corrected the problem, nor will it reverse this broader social trend. Policing must explore new ways to think

> ...agencies employing bureaucratic government structures risk being rendered incapable of addressing their core missions.

> *   *   *

about personnel systems, recruitment, hiring, training, culture, and internal operations. Policing cannot force the modern labor force to fit into a historical organizational model. The profession must find an organizational design that will attract bright, competent, and capable people and will encourage them to continue to work in policing.

Crime, public safety, and homeland security are becoming increasingly complex. Police agencies are being asked to serve an expanding role in society and to shoulder a growing list of mandates. New tools and resources are accompanying this trend. This includes increasing use of analysis and analytics to inform the understanding of crime, disorder, and social problems. It includes greater collaboration with private interests that can provide expertise unavailable within policing personnel. It includes greater partnerships with non-police personnel and organizations to enact solutions that will work.

Above all else, policing needs real leadership. Herman Goldstein once wrote a scathing critique of leadership in American policing; his observations centered on the lack of true leadership, courage, innovation, and forward thinking by police personnel and within police organizations.[1] Changes in the past half-century have, regrettably, been quite minimal. The policing profession continues to systematically suppress innovative ideas and creative thinking, insisting instead on reinforcing tradition and conformist thinking. While the profession develops competent supervisors and administrators, in the future policing will need courageous leaders to remain viable.

What are the future solutions to these daunting circumstances? No one knows. However, this uncertainty cannot be used to justify inaction and a continuation of current operational strategies. Discourse and dialogue are needed; the conversation cannot be limited to policing executives, scholars, or policy makers. Bold and innovative ideas are needed. Courageous leadership is needed. Experimental efforts must be initiated, and we must be prepared for many of those efforts to fail. If the policing profession remains passive and reactive in shaping its own future, the result will be increasing irrelevance for the police and greater vulnerability for communities and citizens. The policing profession must mobilize itself to shape its own future in a way that does not simply seek to preserve a mythical image of bygone days.

I make these observations with all due respect for American policing and its leaders. But I also make these observations as someone who works in another public sector realm that has been undergoing fundamental changes and challenges to historical assumptions. Simply stated, education officials in this nation have failed to show the vision, courage, and true leadership to navigate current challenges to higher education. Policing must do better. ★

Joseph A. Schafer is chair of the Department of Criminology and Criminal Justice at Southern Illinois University, Carbondale. He holds a bachelor's degree from the University of Northern Iowa and a master's and doctorate from Michigan State University. Schafer is a former president of Police Futurists International (PFI), a member of the PFI/FBI Futures Working Group, and a member of the FBI Terrorism Research and Analysis Program. He has served as a visiting scholar with the Behavioral Science Unit at the FBI National Academy and as a visiting fellow with the Centre of Excellence in Policing and Security in Australia. He has published widely on futures issues in policing, police leadership, organizational change, police innovation, police operations, and citizen perceptions of crime, safety, and policing.

Endnotes

1. Goldstein, Herman, *Policing a Free Society* (New York: HarperCollins, 1977).

★ ★ ★

Saving Our Own through Peer Review: A Prescription for Improved Law Enforcement Safety

by Alexander L. Eastman

Too often in law enforcement, when bad outcomes occur, such as death or serious injury to one of our own, law enforcement agencies burrow themselves in the investigation and legal aspects of the consequences. We rarely, if ever, study these incidents in detail with the goal of crafting lessons learned for others to review and subsequently avoid making similar mistakes. Consider almost any of the high-profile murders of U.S. law enforcement officers over the last few years—precious few of these tragedies have been studied and translated into a usable format for officers worldwide. Many other professions are well ahead of us in terms of improvements in safety and effectiveness. For the future of policing, this must change quickly.

…law enforcement lacks a robust national capacity to capture all injuries, analyze trends, and rapidly make recommendations that can be broadcast nationwide.

★ ★ ★

For a poignant example, we need only to look to the medical community. Medical errors—those that harm patients—have received an incredible amount of attention over the last decade. There have been articles not only in scientific journals and medical texts but also in most major U.S. newspapers and magazines. In order to combat these errors and eliminate the real harm that was occurring to patients, doctors, hospitals, and health systems have had to renew focus on maximizing clinical safety and effectiveness. No longer is simple patient care sufficient—that same care must now be timely, efficient, and, most important, safe and free from preventable error. These improvements in healthcare safety and effectiveness started with an analysis of the problem, continued with applying the results of that analysis to present-day bad outcomes through a peer-review process, and culminated with an explosion of publications and marketing of novel programs that work. Meaningful future improvements in law enforcement officer safety will require a paradigm shift; law enforcement administrators must move toward the medical model of less-than-optimal outcome analysis rather than tradition-based models of local investigation and avoiding the tough, performance-improvement issues that desperately need to be discussed.

Officer safety is perhaps the most overused, abused term in law enforcement publications, new protocols, and novel programs over the last five years. An analysis of the immense dollars spent under the umbrella of law enforcement officer safety programs would be nearly impossible given the magnitude and breadth of activities that would be included but likely would yield disappointing results. Many of the programs advocated and implemented over the last several years have not done enough to actually improve law enforcement safety while simultaneously garnering disproportionate attention and resources from the law enforcement community and its leaders.

To make policing safer in 2022, the process must begin with an understanding of the present problem. While the FBI's Law Enforcement Officers Killed and Assaulted dataset and the National Law Enforcement Officers Memorial Foundation both have made attempts to evaluate and characterize officer fatalities, these deaths represent only a small fraction of officers seriously injured in the line of duty each year. Neither of these groups, nor any other out there today, can succinctly and accurately answer the question of how and, more important, why U.S. law enforcement officers are sustaining injuries—a critical first step in determining how to truly improve officer safety.

More recently and moving toward beginning to correct this deficit in our present knowledge, the International Association of Chiefs of Police has published results from its *Reducing Officer Injuries: Developing Policy Responses*—a study that examined 18 U.S. law enforcement agencies employing 9,746 officers (approximately a 1% sample of officers). The study looked at more than 1,200 injuries sustained during the one-year period. The analysis of these injuries is the first step toward meaningful safety improvement.

While many of the injuries studied were minor, two clear trends emerged. First, and most practical, law enforcement training in injury mitigation, health, and wellness has lagged behind other topics. Second, and likely more important, law enforcement lacks a robust national capacity to capture all injuries, analyze trends, and rapidly make recommendations that can be broadcast nationwide. Until we take steps to correct this deficiency, not only will we remain behind other public safety professionals but also each solution will remain relatively isolated, ensuring that others may remain at risk to making the same mistake.

In addition to studying outcomes and data, the second key component of the process by which medical safety and effectiveness continues to improve is that of peer review.[1] The idea is simple—when bad things happen in medicine, a group of peer physicians take a look at the facts of the case; review the care provided and decisions made with a tough, introspective examination; and ultimately provide a proscription of some sort to avoid the bad outcome again. This process, critical to the recent profound improvements in

We fundamentally have to change the way we respond to times when we are not at our best.

* * *

medical care effectiveness and safety, is protected from legal discovery, allowing a frank discussion where all facts are laid bare and meaningful change and improvements can be made. Except in cases of egregious negligence, recommendations for improvement are rarely punitive. Instead, the focus is on improvement and avoidance of similar mistakes in the future. Interestingly, the legal protections afforded to this process do not interfere with malpractice claims—as negligent physicians still have to be held accountable—but it allows mistakes to be evaluated and corrected in real time and to be discussed and distributed to others so mistakes are not repeated.

Law enforcement leaders should take steps to emulate this process, to create a way for us to truly analyze and discuss our mistakes without fear of repercussions and reprisal. Following an officer death in the line of duty, criminal and internal investigations occur in every agency. Too often, agencies hide behind these investigations as rationale for not disseminating crucial safety findings that have the potential for meaningful officer safety improvement. Imagine instead, given

115

the above, a concurrent peer review, done by other law enforcement leaders with access to every important fact and detail that generated nonpunitive, nonjudgmental important lessons learned. These could each be distilled into a five-minute presentation and read at roll-calls all over the nation, providing our officers with the knowledge needed to avoid a similar situation in the future. Whatever format these could be disseminated in, the final product is critical for the future of law enforcement safety. We have to achieve this paradigm shift in the way we examine our tragedies and near-misses.

Worldwide, policing looks completely different in many ways than it was even 20 years ago. Yet as law enforcement agencies continue their transition from compartmentalized, isolationist organizations to a more agile, open, interactive model, we as law enforcement leaders must continue to push the proverbial envelope. If the intention is to make meaningful improvements to law enforcement officer safety in the year 2022, we fundamentally have to change the way we respond to times when we are not at our best. The time to emulate some of our peers is overdue—as is the time to create a meaningful, nonpunitive, and robust national peer review process. ★

Alexander L. Eastman, MD, MPH, FACS, is a lieutenant and the deputy medical director of the Dallas (Texas) Police Department and the lead medical officer for the Dallas Police SWAT team. He also serves as the medical director and SRRT surgeon for The University of Texas (UT) System Police. A former firefighter/rescuer in Montgomery County, Maryland, his interests include the prehospital care of the injured, novel methods of hemostasis, cost-effective care, and the interface between medicine, law enforcement, and public health. Eastman is the vice-chair of the Police Physician's Section of the International Association of Chiefs of Police and a member of the U.S. Department of Justice's Officer Safety and Wellness Group. In addition, Eastman is an assistant professor and trauma surgeon in the Division of Burn/Trauma/Critical Care at UT Southwestern Medical Center and the chief of Trauma at Parkland Memorial Hospital. A graduate with distinction of the George Washington University School of Medicine, he completed his general surgery residency and two fellowships at UT Southwestern Medical School/Parkland Memorial Hospital. He is board certified in both general surgery and surgical critical care and holds a master's degree in public health from the UT Health Science Center at Houston.

Endnotes

1. See O'Dowd, Adrian, "Peer Review Must Stay as Guarantee of Quality, Research Leaders Tell MPs," *British Medical Journal* 342 (2011), doi: 10.1136/bmj.d3656.

★ ★ ★

A Labor Perspective on the Value of Our Internal Communities and Collaborative Leadership

by Christopher Tracy

It would be an understatement to say that the consequences of the 2008 economic decline have been felt across the board for American law enforcement. Nevertheless, here we are. Even now, in 2012, the issues we face are not restricted to large agencies or small departments, big cities or rural communities; we have all been forced to adapt in one way or another to the demands of smaller budgets in a relatively compressed period. Papers have already been written detailing the dire effect the economy has had on our profession, not only from a broad, national perspective but also from each of our various local points-of-view.[1] The bottom line is that most, if not all, law enforcement agencies have had to grapple with less resources, smaller budgets, fewer officers, and reduced training—a trend that sets the stage for the evolution of our profession over the next decade and beyond.

…we have to accept that all of us will need to work together, labor along with management…

*   *   *

In order to cope with the new normal brought on by the worst economic conditions of our lifetimes, many opinions will be offered, outlining strategies for how law enforcement ought to be able to do more with less. There are sure to be proposals advocating ways for departments to be (re)structured with fewer commissioned personnel, suggestions for new and innovative ways to target crime and conduct criminal investigations, and thoughts on ways to regionalize or form new partnerships to reduce budgetary constraints. For the foreseeable future, the greatest consideration for many of these proposals will likely be given to those policy and procedural changes that reduce the most cost.

However, no matter what is proposed and ultimately implemented, because of the relative significance of labor costs to overall budgets, the impacts will ultimately trickle down to and be felt the most by the police officers, detectives, and their immediate supervisors—whom I will refer to here after as our internal community—who make up the front lines of public safety.

Unfortunately, the bad economy combined with austerity policies at the federal, state, and local levels, which have universally slashed police budgets, have taken a dramatic toll on officers and put a strain on labor-management relations. That said, no amount of finger-pointing will undo the current situation. With an eye toward the future, we have to accept that all of us will need to work together, labor along with management, with compassion and a belief in the importance of supporting our (internal) community, along with a healthy dose of constructive leadership to steer the way.

As a labor leader, I fully expect to be engaged in a dialogue with management about these issues, prospective solutions, and their impact as we move forward. Rather than focus my thoughts here on particular solutions, however, I would instead like to take a step back to focus on the consequences these brutal economic times have had and will likely continue to have on our internal communities and the need for collaborative leadership to weather the current storm and look to the future.

As law enforcement agencies cope with smaller budgets, we have all likely witnessed first-hand layoffs (real or threatened), early retirements, eliminated positions, non-existent hiring, staffing shortages, scaled-back services, eliminated specialty units, curtailed overtime opportunities, cancelled non-essential training, or some combination thereof.

There have been several unfortunate consequences as a result of these cutbacks, stemming from large reductions in force. For example, large numbers of senior officers are opting to retire early in order to prevent involuntary layoffs. This is troubling because not only are we losing many great officers before we should have but they also are no longer available to serve as mentors for the next generation. In essence, we have lost vast amounts of institutional knowledge representing careers' worth of experience spent honing criminal investigation techniques, forging relationships in the community, and gathering intelligence on neighborhoods and criminals without having much of a cohesive succession plan in place.

Another consequence is the loss of coveted positions on many of the specialty, proactive units as school resource officers, traffic/motorcycle officers, gang unit, narcotics/vice, and community-based liaison officer programs are reduced or dismantled to save money. These losses will likely have a significant public impact, as these programs have a demonstrated track record of reducing crime and amplifying the effectiveness of patrol as force multipliers. In addition, losing these programs will surely have a negative impact on morale because those positions are highly sought after and many of those eliminated positions resulted in the involuntary transfer of an officer to another assignment.

Beyond those losses, however, perhaps the worst consequence of the current economic crisis is its effect on relationships within our internal communities. Not only has the current economic downturn caused

…we are losing a great many officers before we should…

* * *

untold amounts of stress by increasing the likelihood of forced layoffs and reduced incomes (and there still does not appear to be any sign of real economic recovery on the horizon), but the ongoing nature of the uncertainty has also placed undo emphasis on two possible yet competing solutions: either reduced wages or mandatory layoffs. When framed as an either/or, this type of budget mitigation conversation pits junior officers against senior officers. The ensuing rift is based largely on the competing interests of job preservation against the consequences of wage concessions affecting earning potential and retirement income, with both sides assuming the other is unsympathetic to their individual plights. Despite the fact that alternative solutions might be negotiable, tensions run high when perspectives are restricted to extreme points of view.

Divisions along these lines within our community tear at the very fabric of internal cohesion and sense of community. The problem is then exacerbated by the protracted nature of this economic downturn and the continued uncertainty that has the cumulative effect of sapping morale. In addition, there is a growing hostility due to budget slashing, force reductions, and departmental reorganization decisions that have caused the internal community to increasingly

Put another way, "united we stand, divided we fall."

*   *   *

distrust management's decisions. This feeds into the "us versus them" mentality, and the longer the depressed economy continues to fester, the longer these feelings will persist.

We need to proceed cautiously. A carefully considered, measured approach is critical. Giving in to outrage—pointing the finger and blaming others, either directly or through the media—may satisfy some primal need for instant gratification, but it is unlikely to foster an atmosphere conducive to meaningful, open dialogue and constructive negotiation to advance long-term goals. How then can we focus our efforts to achieve results that are responsive to the needs of our internal communities?

As we consider the way forward, let us start by re-examining the philosophy of community policing and its three key components: organizational transformation (which includes agency management and labor relations), community partnerships, and problem solving.[2] If we view each of our organizations through the lens of the other two components, then the most effective way to address the consequences of the depressed economy is to focus on the need for forging and maintaining internal community partnerships between labor and management as an integral part of effective problem solving. Put another way, "united we stand, divided we fall."

One of the keys to building a bridge to the future (even with our internal communities in a state of turmoil) is having engaged leadership dedicated to collaborative problem solving. To be truly collaborative, both labor and management must be willing to forge long-term relationships, maintain open lines of communication, and invest in ways to negotiate for mutually agreeable outcomes. From a labor perspective, we are arguably far more likely to achieve our goals—such as improving the quality of life for our members—if we focus on working constructively with management.

On the other hand, progress is likely to stagnate or evaporate entirely in the event union leadership adopts a less constructive mentality that boxes management into a defensive corner, for example, by getting caught up in petty squabbles that may benefit only a few members, by arbitrarily exerting its authority unnecessarily, or by obstructing management at every turn.[3] Consequently, given the fragility of the economy, the impacts to internal communities within our law enforcement agencies, and the unique role unions have as the advocate for those internal communities, the stage is set for collaborative union leadership to take charge of shaping a positive trajectory for the future of our profession.

Let me conclude by saying that the next decade is up to all and each of us, whether we be an agency director, chief of police, union president, or patrol officer.

Where we go as a profession from this point forward depends on us recognizing the value of community and collaboration. We need to focus not on blame, outrage, or finger-pointing; instead we need to work together to build the framework for our future, whatever it and the economy brings, by doing what we in law enforcement do: adapt, improvise, and overcome.

Our future, our reputation, indeed our very legacy will be forged, in part, on whether we convince the public we are capable of taking care of each other.

After all, why would anyone trust us to protect and serve if the law enforcement community cannot work together and take care of one another?

We need to get this right. Forget "Too Big to Fail." Our motto as we build to the future ought to be that law enforcement is "Too Important to Fail." The way forward is together as a community, collaboratively. Here we go… ★

Christopher Tracy is a police officer with the Tacoma (Washington) Police Department. He is currently assigned as the administrative officer in the Special Investigations section. He also serves as the vice president of Tacoma Police Union Local No. 6, which represents more than 330 rank and file police officers, detectives, and sergeants. Prior to getting his start in law enforcement, Tracy was an attorney, initially working as an intellectual property litigator for a large international law firm based in Seattle, Washington, and later as an in-house attorney for a global health initiative non-profit. He has a bachelor's degree in cell and molecular biology with a minor in Norwegian from the University of Washington and a law degree from Saint Louis University in Missouri. When he has free time, Tracy enjoys playing golf, reading, cooking, and spending time with family and friends.

Endnotes

1. See *The Impact of the Economic Downturn on American Police Agencies* (Washington, D.C.: U.S. Department of Justice, Office of Community Oriented Policing Services, 2011); Derby-McCurtain, Tarna, et al., *Community Policing Strategies and Effectiveness in Reducing Crime: A Position Paper to the Tacoma City Council* (University of Washington, Tacoma, 2012), paper available upon request at www.tacoma.uw.edu/news/cuts-police-could-compromise-future-safety-budgets.

2. *Community Policing Defined* (Washington, D.C.: U.S. Department of Justice, Office of Community Oriented Policing Services, 2009).

3. I do not mean to suggest that collaborative union leadership means that every decision made by management must be deferred to absolutely. There will be times when labor and management will disagree. In such times, it may become necessary to consider the available alternative dispute resolution tools—including, where applicable, filing grievances, arbitrating claims, and resorting to unfair labor practice claims—to resolve disagreements. In general, though, collaborative relationships would utilize such alternatives only as a matter of last resort, and only after efforts to conciliate jointly have proven to be fruitless.

★ ★ ★

Ending the Monopoly of Tradition

by Edward F. Davis

Ten years is a short time in terms of policing. It is difficult to anticipate any change in a business or organization so steeped in tradition and practices that so define our culture. But today is a unique time in world history. Economic forces are changing long-held beliefs. Technological leaps have given us new tools to utilize. Finally, police have learned much in the past two decades. A better relationship with academia combined with a willingness to experiment with tactics has moved policing back toward the fundamentals espoused by Sir Robert Peel. We are more focused on prevention, and we are working more in partnership with the community. These experiments and better-informed teachings have helped drive down crime and increase trust between the police and the community.

A police force for only those who cannot afford their own protection is in no position to expect ever-increasing tax funding.

*   *   *

Union management responsibility

Great plans, however, mean nothing without the consent and cooperation of the officer on the street. Union relationships are more important than ever, considering cutbacks our service endured over the past five years. These factors should inform police negotiations in the next decade. Reductions in available tax dollars will continue to be a priority for political leaders, a priority driven by public expectations. Hard decisions on staffing and benefits must be made. I am hopeful that unions and management can work together in crafting solutions that will reduce the tax burden, without harming individual officers. Police officers deserve a proper compensation package and retirement benefits. Union and management can work together to educate the community on the risks officers face, especially long-term effects on health, stress, and premature death. The public understands its responsibility to veterans and rightfully so. Police leaders need to draw the public's attention to the plight of the police.

I foresee unions concentrating more on core benefits and less on their agenda of organizational control. This is a simple matter of priority. But giving management more control of internal processes will make the police more responsive to the community at a time when community support of police is vital.

An indisputable fact hovers over these negotiations. The private security industry grows each year. According to the Bureau of Justice Statistics, 19 to 34 billion dollars are spent in the United States by people who desire safety. The police need to access these nontax dollars. A police union and management partnership that enters the competitive bidding process will force the police to become cost effective.

We can no longer afford to rely on a monopoly based on tradition. Those who still believe the police are not in direct competition with the private sector are deluding themselves. Our training is superior, and we have the edge with statutory authority and our unique responsibility to all the people. But these are tenuous facts to rely on. The people have already voted on this issue with their pocketbook. We need to recognize this fact and access a portion of those private dollars through competition. A police force for only those who cannot afford their own protection is in no position to expect ever-increasing tax funding.

Better harnessing of technology for police
Proliferation of miniature video systems and cell phones

Concerned about intrusions on their own privacy, the police have been slow to accept personal video systems. However, the use of miniature video systems and cell phones has been prolific. The police will view this development as beneficial for law enforcement over the next 10 years. Police vendors will develop cameras imbedded in radio equipment that police will use to document any controversial encounter. This technology will assist the police against illegitimate claims of police brutality or bad acts. Initially viewing cameras as an intrusion, officers cleared over time by videos already prevalent in public spaces will see the benefit to having their own cameras.

Similar to recent court decisions regarding the interrogation of suspects, there will be a negative presumption by the court if police do not have film and audio to back up their claims. At the same time, this development will ensure police officers act in accordance with policies, procedures, and regulations. Fewer resources devoted to internal investigations will result.

Virtual policing

Technology will play an important role in how police perform their patrol. The lessons we have learned in the battlefield during the last two wars in Iraq and Afghanistan have resulted in computer systems that create complete situational awareness for troops. These systems can be easily adapted to policing. Soon, police officers on patrol will view a running map that shows threats, gun permit locations, problem properties, the location of probationers' and parolees' residences, and the location of those who are on GPSs. This information and more will be streamed in real time, eliminating the step of officers having to request it.

...technology will assist the police against illegitimate claims of police brutality or bad acts.

* * *

GPS—an alternative to incarceration

The use of GPSs on suspects will be viewed by courts as an attractive and inexpensive addition to incarceration. These systems will drastically reduce crime rates. Based on the knowledge that a small number of people commit a large number of crimes, better surveillance of this small population will result in added efficiencies for the prevention of crime. In Boston today, ShotSpotter technology is overlaid with probationers' GPS locations, resulting in instant resolution to shooting incidents.

Use of data

Millions of crimes go unsolved in the United States each year. More extensive use of DNA in misdemeanor cases, for example, will increase clearance rates. Effective use of video from the millions of systems currently deployed nationwide will accomplish the same goal. Black box technology in motor vehicles is another underutilized investigative lead. There is simply not enough time or money to investigate fully all but the most serious of crimes.

In 10 years, DNA will be cheaper and easier to use. Data clouds containing massive amounts of video and inputs from plate readers and GPSs will be combined and lead to fast resolution of crime. Much debate is needed to balance the extent of data mining and privacy concerns and to ensure the public is free of victimization by criminals and government intrusion.

The combination of economic forces, technology, and smarter policing will coalesce into different practices for policing in 10 short years. These factors are indisputable. The only question is how far management and labor will go to achieve logical change that is beneficial to the community and the police. We need to remember that the police are the public and the public, the police. Mindful of the great management and union leaders currently in policing, I am optimistic for the future. ★

Edward F. Davis is the 40th police commissioner of the city of Boston. He was sworn in by Mayor Menino on December 4, 2006. As police commissioner, Davis has recommitted the agency to community policing and combined it with predictive policing. He created and implemented Safe Street Teams—engaging officers in community oriented policing in hot spot areas throughout the city—and reinvigorated "Operation Ceasefire" to reduce gang violence. From 2006 through 2011, the city of Boston experienced a 25% decrease in Part I Crime. Prior to becoming commissioner of the Boston Police Department, Davis served as the superintendent of police in Lowell, Massachusetts, for 12 years. During that time, the city of Lowell realized a 60% reduction in Part I Crime. Commissioner Davis is the recipient of numerous awards, including the National Leadership Award (2002) from the Police Executive Research Forum and the Hundred Club of Massachusetts' 2011 Humanitarian Award. He was also the recipient of the NIJ Pickett Fellowship and attended the Harvard Kennedy School, John F. Kennedy School of Government's program for Senior Executives in State and Local Government. A founding member of the Massachusetts Major City Chiefs, Davis serves on the association's board of directors, as well as that of the Police Executive Research Forum. He holds a bachelor's and master's degree in criminal justice from Southern New Hampshire University (formerly New Hampshire College) in Manchester, New Hampshire, and from Anna Maria College in Paxton, Massachusetts, respectively.

★ ★ ★

Reflections on the Eve of My Retirement: A Letter from the Future

by Chris Cognac

I think back to the days when I started working as a rookie street cop in 1992. The trust in the police was at an all time low; the riots that resulted from the Rodney King beating verdict had just ended. Crack cocaine was invading the streets and housing projects of America's inner cities. Police departments were engaged in a full on battle for the streets against the gangs that killed and intimidated those who opposed them.

The gangs were bold; attacks on police officers and even on police stations themselves skyrocketed. Officers were forced to put up bullet proof glass in the station lobbies, purchase armored vehicles to serve warrants, and retreat to the relative safety of the police car. It was "us versus them," and we determined to take everyone we could to jail and to "win" no matter what the cost.

127

The era of crime fighting and "force multiplying" through social media was upon us.

* * *

Then there was a new trend called the "Internet," and everyone was on it. People were communicating with other people all around the world in chat rooms and bulletin boards. Cellular phones became affordable and included cameras on every phone. People began to use cell phone cameras to record the police whenever they could, hoping to catch a rogue officer so they could send it to the media. Special interest groups and people with hidden agendas began to set up officers by using hidden video cameras and microphones, hoping to create an incident in which they could file a lawsuit to further their cause. Once these videos that were often edited to fit the needs of a group were made public, it further drove a wedge between the police and the community. Where once the public trusted the word of individual police officers, there was now suspicion and the thought of deception on the part of the police. The police in general were still stuck in the 1980s and took the defensive posture of "no comment."

Entering the second decade of the new millennium, the police as a whole began to examine how they could do things better and how they could become more approachable and trusted using the new technology available to them, such as social media like Facebook and YouTube. Individual officers and units began to reach out to the public and educate them about crime prevention, disaster preparedness, and even how to organize a neighborhood watch group using a new thing called Twitter. Speaking of Twitter, police began to use it as a way to instantly notify the local community of breaking issues, such as street closures or major crime trends and suspect descriptions. This resulted in building trust within the community, as it empowered the ordinary citizen to help fight crime. All of a sudden, the long-lost bonds between the police and community were being re-established after many years of neglect and mistrust. The era of crime fighting and "force multiplying" through social media was upon us.

The one constant that had not changed was the police car. The traditional police vehicle was a big Ford or Chevy V-8 loaded with so much equipment that just getting in and out of one for years was causing a multitude of work-related back injuries for officers around the country. Gasoline was $4.50 a gallon and not getting any cheaper, and the cost of replacing a vehicle was approaching $60,000 by the middle part of the decade. Something needed to change.

A few forward-thinking police departments teamed up with electric vehicle manufacturers, such as Segway, Tesla, and Brammo, to help design the future of transportation for police. The transition from gasoline to electric-powered vehicles was not an easy one. In the beginning, many officers were reluctant to break away from the safety of what they had always known and were used to. The electric motorcycles looked different; they were not as cool as the Harley-Davidsons or BMWs that motor officers had ridden since the advent of the modern motor officer. The Tesla electric vehicles used to be able to go only 150 miles on a charge and barely went 100 mph, which is why they were phased into unmarked detective units for the first few years. It took a few years, but the cost savings in fuel and maintenance alone prompted the remaining police agencies to give up gasoline vehicles and not only go green for the environment but also go green for budgets!

In the third decade of my career I observed that officers were being required to carry more and more equipment to include a multitude of less-lethal options, audio as well as video recording devices, and handheld electronic devices in place of the traditional mobile data terminal that went away with the gasoline vehicles. The workplace injuries began to increase due to the amount of equipment carried and the no-place-to-carry-it problem of the traditional Sam Browne belt.

The police uniform as we knew it was no longer practical, so, like with the switch to electric vehicles, we switched to a more functional uniform for patrol officers (while still keeping tradition alive in the dress uniform). Gone was the 30 pounds of gear around the waistline of an officer, replaced by the external ballistic vest with load-distributing technology that allowed officers more freedom of movement and reduced injuries (on a drastic scale as we now know). The vest was fitted with the appropriate electronic

> # In the beginning, many officers were reluctant to break away from the safety of what they had always known…

* * *

equipment, and the firearm and holster moved from the "hip placement" to a more ergonomically friendly thigh holster.

The smart gun started to be implemented across the nation. The guns use a fingerprint-recognition safety system that allows the officer to fire the weapon only when the gun recognizes the officer's fingerprints. I am proud to say that since this has been implemented, no officer has been killed in the line of duty with his or her own weapon. I understand that the next generation of firearms will have a built-in less-lethal option, but I won't be around to test that one (although it is sure to impress).

I have seen a lot of things change in my 30 years on the job. I went from a young rookie with just a badge and a gun. It was "us versus them;" take 'em to jail and go home was the motto. Now in 2022, I am seasoned and, so I like to think, a wise veteran cop who realizes that the police need to think outside the box, partner with the people they serve, and look for better ways to do things, as there is always room for improvement.

I think of the grizzled crusty street cops I looked up to when I was 24 and working the night shift. We thought they knew it all (and so did they). I wonder what the 24–year-old rookie thinks of me and my peers now? Do they think we know it all? I know that we are quite aware we don't!

When those kids are my age, what will they be like in 2052? Will they fly hover cars and use laser beams? It's possible, that's one thing I know for sure, because if you would have told a 24-year-old me what kind of technology and equipment the 54-year-old me is using, I never would have believed you.

Be safe, and don't forget the old retired guys like me! ★

Chris Cognac is a 20-year veteran of the Hawthorne (California) Police Department. He is the sergeant currently assigned to the Community Affairs Unit but has served in numerous capacities from uniform patrol, to sexual assault and crimes against children detective, to cooperative resource unit, to aviation bureau, to undercover narcotics supervisor. Cognac is a true believer in the ability of individual officers making a difference in the communities they serve. He uses his networking and communication skills as a force multiplier, putting people who want to help the community with those in need of an opportunity. Most recently, he has begun to take the simple concept of "Coffee with a Cop" nationwide. He has assisted officers and police departments across the country in implementing their own events that aim to build good communications and trust within those communities. Cognac is a graduate of the Delinquency Control Institute at the University of Southern California. In his spare time, he is a food and travel writer for magazines and newspapers and develops new food television concepts. He also hosted his own Food Network TV show, *The Hungry Detective*.

★ ★ ★

Commonly Used Terms

Association of Public-Safety Communications Officials International (APCO International)

Bureau of Justice Assistance (BJA)

closed-circuit television (CCTV)

community oriented policing (COP)

computer-aided dispatch (CAD)

crime prevention through environmental design (CPTED)

Criminal Justice Information Services (CJIS)

Data-Driven Approach to Crime and Traffic Safety (DDACTS)

Department of Justice (DOJ)

Department of Motor Vehicle (DMV)

electronic control weapons (ECW)

Federal Bureau of Investigation (FBI)

Global Justice Information Sharing Initiative (Global)

intelligence-led policing (ILP)

International Association of Chiefs of Police (IACP)

International Association of Fire Chiefs (IAFC)

International Organization of Standardization (ISO)

Law Enforcement Officers Killed and Assaulted (LEOKA)

Major City Chiefs Association (MCCA)

mobile data terminal (MDT)

National Association of State EMS Officials (NASEMSO)

National Crime Information Center (NCIC)

National Executive Institute Associates (NEIA)

National Incident-Based Reporting System (NIBRS)

National Information Exchange Model (NIEM)

National Intelligence Criminal Service (NICS)

National Intelligence Model (NIM)

National Law Enforcement Officers Memorial Foundation (NLEOMF)

National League of Cities (NLC)

National Public Safety Telecommunications Council (NPSTC)

National Sheriffs' Association (NSA)

Nationwide Suspicious Activity Reporting Initiative (NSI)

Office of Community Oriented Policing Services
(COPS Office)

Office of Justice Programs (OJP)

Police Executive Research Forum (PERF)

Police Training Officer (PTO) program

problem-oriented policing (POP)

public safety answering points (PSAP)

records management system (RMS)

special weapons and tactics (SWAT)

Suspicious Activity Reporting (SAR)

Uniformed Crime Report (UCR)

★ ★ ★

About the COPS Office

The Office of Community Oriented Policing Services (COPS Office) is the component of the U.S. Department of Justice responsible for advancing the practice of community policing by the nation's state, local, territory, and tribal law enforcement agencies through information and grant resources.

Community policing is a philosophy that promotes organizational strategies that support the systematic use of partnerships and problem-solving techniques, to proactively address the immediate conditions that give rise to public safety issues such as crime, social disorder, and fear of crime.

Rather than simply responding to crimes once they have been committed, community policing concentrates on preventing crime and eliminating the atmosphere of fear it creates. Earning the trust of the community and making those individuals stakeholders in their own safety enables law enforcement to better understand and address both the needs of the community and the factors that contribute to crime.

The COPS Office awards grants to state, local, territory, and tribal law enforcement agencies to hire and train community policing professionals, acquire and deploy cutting-edge crime fighting technologies, and develop and test innovative policing strategies. COPS Office funding also provides training and technical assistance to community members and local government leaders and all levels of law enforcement.

The COPS Office has produced and compiled a broad range of information resources that can help law enforcement better address specific crime and operational issues, and help community leaders better understand how to work cooperatively with their law enforcement agency to reduce crime.

- Since 1994, the COPS Office has invested nearly $14 billion to add community policing officers to the nation's streets, enhance crime fighting technology, support crime prevention initiatives, and provide training and technical assistance to help advance community policing.

- By the end of FY2011, the COPS Office has funded approximately 123,000 additional officers to more than 13,000 of the nation's 18,000 law enforcement agencies across the country in small and large jurisdictions alike.

- Nearly 700,000 law enforcement personnel, community members, and government leaders have been trained through COPS Office-funded training organizations.

- As of 2011, the COPS Office has distributed more than 6.6 million topic-specific publications, training curricula, white papers, and resource CDs.

COPS Office resources, covering a wide breadth of community policing topics—from school and campus safety to gang violence—are available, at no cost, through its online Resource Information Center at www.cops.usdoj.gov. This easy-to-navigate website is also the grant application portal, providing access to online application forms. ★

About the Editors

Debra R. Cohen McCullough serves as a senior analyst with the Research and Development division of the COPS Office. In this capacity, she manages federal grants and cooperative agreements for research, training and technical assistance, and publications dedicated to supporting public safety. Her portfolio includes programs designed to ensure the successful implementation of communications technology projects, enhance cultural competency, and improve officer safety. Under her maiden name, Cohen, she is the author of articles highlighting projects on technology, crisis management, information sharing, and police facility architecture. She also manages the development of nationally distributed publications and websites, such as the Law Enforcement Tech Guide series, the technology-focused Issue Briefs, and DiscoverPolicing.org. McCullough played a key role in the office's 311 non-emergency system initiatives and served as interagency liaison for national survey projects. As a singer and songwriter, she became adept at the art of collaboration, the science of coordination, and the use of duct tape. McCullough earned her doctorate and master's degree in criminal justice from the State University of New York at Albany and bachelor's degree in political science from Rider University (formerly Rider College) in New Jersey.

Deborah L. Spence is a supervisory analyst with the Research and Development Division of the COPS Office. In addition to her supervisory duties, she oversees analytical functions relating to grant program development and is the editor-in-chief of the COPS Office e-newsletter, the *Community Policing Dispatch*. She has recently focused her work on the economy and public safety by managing a project on public safety consolidations as well as co-authoring *The Impact of the Economic Downturn on Law Enforcement in America* and *The Relationship Between Economic Conditions, Policing, and Crime Trends*. Prior to joining the COPS Office, Spence worked for the Institute for Law and Justice where she co-authored two COPS Office publications, *Guidelines for Starting and Operating a New Police Department* and *Call Management and Community Policing*. She also worked on several national evaluations of programs created by the Violent Crime Control and Law Enforcement Act of 1994. Spence initially honed her multi-tasking abilities growing up as a competitive figure skater but ultimately traded her blades for books to earn a master's degree in justice, law, and society from American University in addition to a master's degree in modern history from the University of St. Andrews in Scotland.

59635086R00083

Made in the USA
Charleston, SC
10 August 2016